CREATING COMMUNITY

An Every-Member Approach to Ministry in the Local Church

DAVID PRIOR

NAVPRESS

BRINGING TRUTH TO LIFE

NavPress Publishing Group

P.O. Box 35001, Colorado Springs, Colorado 80935

The Navigators is an international Christian organization. Jesus Christ gave His followers the Great
Commission to go and make disciples (Matthew
28:19). The aim of The Navigators is to help fulfill
that commission by multiplying laborers for Christ
in every nation.

NavPress is the publishing ministry of The Navigators. NavPress publications are tools to help
Christians grow. Although publications alone cannot make disciples or change lives, they can help
believers learn biblical discipleship, and apply what
they learn to their lives and ministries.

Library of Congress Catalog Card Number:
   92-85283
ISBN 08910-97139

Cover illustration: Tim Grajek

Some of the anecdotal illustrations in this book are
true to life and are included with the permission
of the persons involved. All other illustrations are
composites of real situations, and any resemblance
to people living or dead is coincidental.

Unless otherwise identified, all Scripture in this
publication is from the *Revised Standard Version Bible*
(RSV), copyright © 1946, 1952, 1971, by the Division
of Christian Education of the National Council
of the Churches of Christ in the USA, used by
permission, all rights reserved. Other versions used
include: the *Holy Bible: New International Version*
(NIV), Copyright © 1973, 1978, 1984, International
Bible Society, used by permission of Zondervan
Bible Publishers; and the *Good News Bible: Today's
English Version* (TEV), copyright © American Bible
Society 1966, 1971, 1976.

Printed in the United States of America

CONTENTS

ACKNOWLEDGMENTS

Although direct quotations are rare in this book, it will be obvious that I owe a great deal to many sources of wisdom and experience—imbibed over the years and absorbed into practical ministry.

I have used specific material in chapter 4—"Keeping It Small"—from two churches: St. Mary's, Upton, in Cheshire, England; and Christ Church, Kenilworth in Cape Town, South Africa. I am most grateful for these contributions.

The painstaking work of producing a final manuscript has been undertaken by several members of St. Michael's, Chester Square, in central London—notably Andrea Court, Angie Poppitt, Morag Scott-Farrar, and Jenny Moores. They have together done a wonderful job and I thank them most warmly.

NavPress has been patient over a long time, putting up with delays due to injury and illness. Special thanks are due to Karen Lee-Thorp, who has encouraged the project from the beginning.

INTRODUCTION

This book contains reflections on twenty-five years in local church ministry, spent mainly in four different places as a pastor, but with many opportunities to see firsthand the life of other churches in different parts of the world.

The four churches have all turned out to involve bringing together people of different backgrounds. The first, in a country commuter town twenty miles south of London, meant a degree of specialization on youth work. The growing numbers of young people presented quite a challenge to more conservative older members of the church. Within the youth club itself we were forced to tackle potentially difficult situations, when local "Mods" and "Rockers" (a 1960s phenomenon including leather jackets and motorcycles) began to take part in club activities.

The second church was part of a large multiracial parish in Cape Town, where our priority was bringing together people of different racial backgrounds in the community life of the church. Again, the distinctive challenge of this was brought by young people, who mixed with growing freedom in the multiracial youth work of the parish.

Then in Oxford we had the more subtle, but equally demanding, task of uniting the student life of the congregation with members from local Oxford life: "town and gown" mix only with great difficulty in such situations.

Now, in central London, we live and work in an area in which the seriously wealthy and the seriously poor exist cheek by jowl within two or three blocks of one another. Within the geographical area served by our parish there live all kinds of people from every conceivable social and cultural background. It is all extremely international and cosmopolitan in character.

All four situations have compelled us to take seriously the plain description in the New Testament of a church comprised of people of all backgrounds and cultures, united in a common allegiance to Jesus Christ as Lord. This shared community life has proved an elusive, yet unavoidable, dream of what could happen in the world of the twentieth century . . . and on into the twenty-first.

In this book I have attempted to draw on all these experiences. I hope that what emerges will encourage more people to see their local church as God's way into the empty, pagan, desperate, violent, and divided lives all around us. The book provides no simple blueprint, but my hope and prayer is that it will stimulate thinking, talking, and action in many local churches nationwide.

The primary launching pad for gathering this material was a two-week series of lectures at Fuller Seminary in Pasadena, California, in January 1990. I had the inestimable privilege of working with seven others from St. Michael's Church, Chester Square, in central London. As a team, we shared our experiences of "Local Church Renewal and Evangelism" with about fifty students in the master of divinity course.

I have much reason to believe that the emphasis of this book—establishing community life in Christ in local churches—is both timely and necessary for congregations of all sizes over all geographic areas. After a long period of improving our professional skills and developing our expertise, leaders (both lay and ordained, full-time and part-time) in local churches are aware that we may well be in danger of losing our corporate soul in gaining a whole new world of qualifications, ideas, gimmicks, programs, and techniques. It would be wonderful if this book could be a catalyst for many local churches to discover, either for the first time or in the joy of recapture, the community life of the Holy Spirit.

CHAPTER ONE

CREATING COMMUNITY

What kind of church do we want? What kind of church does God want? How will we recognize a church that is on the way to being what God wants it to be? If a local church is the means God uses to meet the needs of individuals, what will it look like when it is being useful to God for His purposes? What will it feel like when people come and see it in operation? What will they notice as its identifying marks?

WHAT DO WE WANT?

A True Community

Above all, such a church will have the feel of being *a true community*, a place where people feel they belong, where they are welcomed, accepted, and both challenged and encouraged. Whatever is said and done in such a church will have the goal and the result of building its community life; if what is said and done does not move people in this direction, it will be put on one side.

This becomes clear in the Apostle Paul's insights when writing to the church at Colossae. Having emphasized in chapter 3 how important it is for the Colossian church to "put to death" everything to do with "the old nature" (in sexual, social, and conversational aspects of daily life), the apostle goes on to explain that "the new nature" is actually

9

a corporate experience in which the whole Christian community at Colossae had come to share. This new nature is being constantly renewed — that is, kept new and fresh — by God Himself. It is God, the Creator, who is at work in the church to bring about a new creation after the likeness of Jesus, His Son.

In this new community life of God, "Christ is all, and in all." In other words, each individual member of the church has Christ within him or her, and Christ is everything to the church as a whole: He matters more than anything or anyone; He provides both the model and the inspiration for its life together. When our English translation (accurately) talks of this new nature as "here," it is emphasizing that the life of a local church, whether in Colossae or Chicago, is first and foremost a place of renewed community life, where God is reproducing the quality of togetherness, integration, and abundant living we see in Jesus Christ. It will also become more and more a place where the family life of the Godhead (Father, Son, and Holy Spirit) is visible and experienced.

No Barriers
One main feature of the local church in which the renewing activity of God is being released will be *the removal of manmade barriers between people of different racial, cultural, social, and educational backgrounds*. The apostle tells us, "Here there cannot be [literally, "is not"] Greek and Jew, circumcised and uncircumcised, barbarian, Scythian, slave, free man" (Colossians 3:11). Human beings, today as always, create groups in which they feel safe with people of their own kind. This is second nature to us. But it is the "old nature." Have we realized that a fundamental characteristic of God's work in creating the community life of the local church is to remove the barriers and, in and through Christ, to create something totally new and different?

One mark, therefore, of a church moving in the Spirit is

the way people of different backgrounds experience both a sense of belonging and a growing freedom to relate to one another in Christ.

Is that the kind of church we want and are gradually becoming? Is Christ the One in whom the church members find their oneness, their purpose, their identity, and their inspiration? Or do these important realities have their source in something or someone less than Christ?

Paul is clearly concerned that the church at Colossae build its community life in a way that transcends superficial, natural, purely human norms. Twice in the same passage he talks about what goes on "in your hearts." He wants the peace of Christ to rule in the people's hearts; he wants the church's worship to be characterized by thankfulness in their hearts to God. God alone looks at and gets through to the hearts of the church members. It is very common for a church to have everything together superficially—the right programs, the necessary buildings, the appropriate leadership, the good reputation in the vicinity—but it is all on the surface: people's hearts remain untouched and unchanged.

Gratitude
One distinctive hallmark of a local church that is building community life after the likeness of Christ is *sheer, uncomplicated thankfulness*. Whenever Paul thought about the church at Colossae, which he had never met or visited, he found himself thanking God for them (1:3)—and asking God that they would increasingly become a people "giving thanks to the Father" (1:12). Indeed, he urges them to be a people "abounding in thanksgiving" (2:7). Then, in chapter 3, he exhorts them to be thankful three times in successive verses (15-17).

Do we want a grateful church? Is that our aim for our church? So many churches seem short on thankfulness and long on whining and moaning. Is gratitude the characteristic

quality of our life together? A critical spirit soon disman-
tles any experience of community. Many people have left a
church because the attitudes prevalent in it are no different
from those in any other group or society. Who needs more
grumbling, more harshness, more churlishness?

It is apparent from Paul's words to the Colossian Christians that a thankful church is not a banal, trite, superficial
place of empty pleasantries: "Let the word of Christ dwell
in you richly, teach and admonish one another in all wisdom" (3:16). The truth is taught, shared, and lived—with
thanksgiving. This affects conversation, behavior, relationships, decision making, all of which are to express the
privilege and the distinctiveness of being "God's chosen
ones." Those chosen by God are "holy and beloved"—holy
because beloved; that is, we are distinctive because we know
we are loved with steadfast, everlasting love and therefore
we gratefully live out new lives in the assurance that that
love will never let us go.

What kind of church do we want? It is important to ask
the question again. Do we want a church where people of
different backgrounds and approaches can meet and mix?
Do we want a church where the most obvious quality is
sheer gratitude? Do we want a church in which Christ is
everything, where the peace of Christ matters more than
keeping the peace at all costs, where the Word of Christ has
taken up residence in people's inner being and is not simply
listened to but acted on, where the name of Christ is the
name most mentioned and revered? Do we want a church
that is manifestly the work of God and equally clearly *not*
the achievement of human beings? Do we want a church
in which the very character and nature of Christ is being
expressed in the way its members are growing individually
and in the way they treat one another? It is relatively simple
to mouth "Yes" to all these questions. It is quite a different
matter to implement priorities and patterns of behavior that
demonstrate we really mean business.

GLASNOST

Is there any basic attitude that can get us moving in the right direction? I believe there is, and the Russians have a word for it—*glasnost*, or "openness." We need more *glasnost* in the church, and the *glasnost* needs to be embraced in every aspect of life, neither selectively nor halfheartedly. Openness is not a state we achieve, but an attitude we adopt. *It is, by definition, not being closed to any possibility, any development, any situation, any person.* To build Christian community life in a local church, we require openness in many directions. In the rest of this book different aspects of such openness will be examined in detail, but for the moment let us consider them in an overall perspective.

Open to God

First and foremost, we need to be open to God. It is fashionable to see such openness to God in terms of openness to life and to people—that is, to play down the reality of a personal, intimate, one-to-one relationship with God. But the essence of God's "new covenant" in Jesus Christ through the Holy Spirit is a direct relationship between each individual and the Creator. Am I open to that relationship—open to God at work within me, to make Himself known to me, to go on making Himself known more and more to me? Do I look for Him, listen to Him, long to be with Him? Have I come to recognize the uniquely distinctive way He speaks to me and makes known to me His heart, His mind, His will? Am I open to His love, His light, His truth, His word? Have I come to know Him well enough to appreciate that I have hardly begun to know Him at all? Does this awareness create a desire, a determination to press on to know Him better?

This openness to God is particularly necessary in two contexts—stress and success. The stress may be caused by the pressures of responsibility, illness, or bereavement, by failure or by sin, by ill treatment from others, or by force of circumstances in daily life. Do we remain open to God at such times, or do we close up and effectively exclude Him from relevance to our situation? When it comes to life in the local church, the way such openness to God in times of stress is tackled will either strengthen or sap its community life. Its leaders clearly have a major responsibility in this, as in every area, and we will be looking in detail at the principles of leadership in later chapters.

The first letter of the Apostle Peter—to scattered Christian communities in the Roman provinces of the northeastern Mediterranean—was written to encourage local churches facing significant times of stress to remain open to God. It remains a valuable primer for local churches in such situations.

Equally, a local church must fight to remain open to God in times of success. When goals are being achieved and there is visible evidence of God's blessing, it is very easy to become closed to God. A church that has it all together— or thinks it has—can effectively shut its ears and heart to God. That is, classically, what happened to the church at Laodicea, a prosperous town a few miles downstream from Colossae on the river Lycus. The Laodicean church reckoned it had reached the point of needing nothing: it had spiritually prospered and was a great success. It had stopped listening to God and learning from God (Revelation 3:14-21). From personal experience of outward success, both in the churches where I have been in leadership and in churches where I have been asked to advise on my travels, it is clear to me that successful churches find it very hard to remain open to God.

Open to One Another

This openness is also expressed in the way we live with one another, both in the local church and in the neighborhood. For example, we commonly hear of churches where "it is impossible to get to know anyone at any depth," where newcomers find barriers around established groupings, where regular members scarcely know anything about what is going on in others' hearts and homes, where almost by silent agreement nobody moves beyond the superficial and the insignificant. To be open with one another is axiomatic in the community life of God's people—open to failure, open to collapse and weakness, open to needs and problems. This involves being open *with* others about our failures, weaknesses, and needs; it also involves being open *to* others in their failures, weaknesses, and needs. Because we all have limited resources and specific thresholds when it comes to such openness, we need (as we will examine later) to accept the value of a limited sphere where we operate in the spirit of *glasnost*.

Open to Outsiders

For many churches a bigger challenge is to build openness with those outside the life of the church altogether, those with different beliefs or without any faith at all. It is a call we ignore to our impoverishment, because the model shown in Jesus Christ, which God is seeking to express again in each local church, was fundamentally one of openness to those who had no time or love for Him. He came to seek and save the lost, that is, those without God and without hope in the world. He was so open to them that He was eventually crucified by them and for them.

A church that is building its life as a *Christian* community will live in a similar openness with those who are "outside." Experience shows that this is no simple or cheap matter. Especially in the secularized paganism of the West, openness to those who have no faith in Christ requires thorough and costly identification with the way they experience lostness—which may be with pain or pleasure, which may have brought confusion or certainty. Very few churches with a strong community life within their fellowship have effectively tackled this kind of *glasnost*.

As we will see in chapter 9, it is important to discover places and opportunities of *access* from outside to inside. At present the life of a church is often light years away from the world of the outsider. It requires a massive effort of courage and even separation to step inside, because the life of the church is virtually inaccessible. This is true both socially and in basic presuppositions about daily living.

Too often, Christians are defensive and judgmental when surrounded by other creeds and different convictions. This defensiveness leads either to wishy-washy compromise on basic biblical truth, or to aggressive pontification that is unable to listen, let alone enter into genuine conversation about matters of life and death. There is an urgent need for a thorough understanding and presentation of a specifically *Christian* perspective—not in any adversarial or polemical mode, but in open statement of Christian thinking in a world that is characterized by both paganism and pluralism.

In the trade, this expression of theological openness is called apologetics and dialogue. Both tend to have become dirty words, but both are integral to true openness in a post-Christian and multicultural society. The world of the twenty-first century is not going to get any less pagan or heterogeneous. The church that retreats into itself will become increasingly irrelevant and odd. It will then be a huge temptation to think that our irrelevance and oddness is *their* fault, not *ours*.

If a local church is seriously intending to be open to those outside, it will need to tackle the following question: What is our geographical target area? In more settled and less mobile days, there was no such question to be asked. People lived, worked, played, and socialized in their local community. Each village or town had its own church building—or several buildings. The geographical situation of the building witnessed to its central role in the life of the community. If members of that community did not take part in the life of their local church, they took part in nothing

Christian. The invention of the car changed all that. Now it is normal for a person to sleep in one community, work in another, play in a third, and socialize in all three, if not a fourth. If a local church is to be open to outsiders, it has to ask fundamental questions about what it perceives to be its true neighborhood. To what extent are we cutting the nerve of effective ministry to outsiders through our domination by the automobile? Easy transport presents many options for churchgoing—and it often becomes just that, that is, church*going* rather than active membership in a *local* church that is having impact in its own community.

Open to Risk and Failure
It will now be clear that true openness to God and to people, both inside and outside the church, necessarily involves openness to change, new ideas, risks, and the unexpected. This is always true of *glasnost*. It is worthwhile for us to think a bit more about these aspects of openness. As Christians we find it surprisingly difficult both to take risks and, even more, to make mistakes. Indeed, we take few risks because we do not like making mistakes. Actually, we may well find that what we tend to call a mistake is not really a mistake at all, but failure. And it is failure we cannot face—so we call it a mistake.

After more than twenty years in pastoral activity, I am clearer now that failure is integral to Christian ministry. It was for Jesus in His ministry: He failed with the young ruler; He failed in Nazareth because of the people's unbelief; He failed with Judas Iscariot; He failed with the bulk of His fellow countrymen; He failed with the religious leadership; He failed with nine of the ten lepers; He failed with Pontius Pilate. In the face of repeated failure, Jesus learned to abide firmly in the love of His Father and to keep His Father's Word.

These events in His ministry were not mistakes. He took the risk of being open with people with the love of

God: many responded favorably, many did not. If, then, we live in the love of God and listen to the Word of God, we will meet constant failure. It will be tempting, because we live in such a results-dominated society, to see failure as reprehensible and therefore to be avoided. One way to avoid failure is to call it a mistake—and then to try to eliminate any mistakes, to make sure we get things right and that we succeed. Many local churches base their activities on such priorities and virtually reject anything that is at all risky, because "we cannot afford to make mistakes."

The terminology that includes "mistakes" suggests a programed approach to the will of God, one that envisages a blueprint in God's workshop that must be copied with complete accuracy. When we take in the liberating truth that God's blueprint is a person, Jesus Christ, not a program, we are freed from a fear of failure; we no longer need to live in fear of getting it wrong and missing out on God's plan for us or for His Church. There is infinite variety in the purposes of God. There is infinite variety in Jesus Christ. God weaves together everything that happens in our lives in order to recreate us in the likeness of His Son.

Let us, then, be open to risk taking and to failure. This will mean being open to the variety of gifts and potential in each member of the local church. It will mean striving to release these gifts into full expression. It will mean a fundamental attitude of each counting others better than himself or herself, believing that the church will become like Christ the more every individual is free to become himself or herself in Christ.

This will mean encouraging the entrepreneurial spirit in individuals. Until I came to London in 1985, I favored a fairly ordered, centrally directed pattern of church life. We looked for steady, reliable-in-the-long-term people to maintain the major work of the church. These folk were entrusted with major responsibilities: They were given specific work to do, were held clearly accountable, and were chosen for their regularity in attendance and their loyalty to those in leadership. Indeed, we saw regular attendance to be the touchstone of loyalty, even its guarantee. The church had to be well-run: i.e., we had to find reliable people to do jobs.

We were probably concerned more that the organized life of the church was in good order, than that the people who are the church were growing spiritually. As Jean Vanier warns us, "A community that is committed to itself, to appearing perfect, stable and secure—rather than to *people*, to their growth and inner freedom, is like a person giving an address who is more interested in the beauty and coherence of the talk rather than in whether the audience can hear and understand it."[1]

The inevitable result of such an approach was that we found ourselves excluding from creative ministry all who could not be present in a consistent way, or who could not undertake to commit themselves over the long haul. In London we soon discovered that such a policy automatically sidelines the majority of committed people. What it took longer to realize was that we were also stifling, if not losing, the spirit of William Carey—"Expect great things from God, attempt great things for God." We were in danger of being safe and sound in a well-ordered church, but of failing to unleash the rich variety of gifting in the body of believers. The fact that we were all the time growing in numbers and reputation was neither here nor there.

So we tried more and more to notice and to use the entrepreneurs in our midst. We want to be open to the distinctive gifts of such people, to give them their head and to encourage them to gather friends around them who share their enthusiasm. We try to help them understand the overall vision and priorities with which the church is fired. We help them work out parameters of operation, patterns of account-ability, and (where appropriate) budgetary considerations. But, in essence, we say, "Get on with it; do it with a few others; see how it goes; this is the person at the center who

will be available to you and to whom you are accountable."
Because entrepreneurs are used to getting, rather than keeping things going, we accept and agree on a fairly limited time
scale. We stress the need to operate together in the love of
Christ. If it doesn't "work," it doesn't work—entrepreneurs
are used to a high-risk factor and failure rate.

This, too, is spiritual *glasnost*. Instead of stifling individual gifting and skill within a centrally controlled system,
the policy is to let it happen freely as people take responsibility for their own insights, ideas, and imagination. Permission is given to experiment, to take risks. It is striking to
discover that such an atmosphere unleashes immense crea-
tivity, in particular in evangelism and in contact with those
outside the church. It also stimulates a richer, more open,
and more profound fellowship among believers.

In particular, church life is gradually transformed from
being a seemingly endless round of meetings to being a
place of meeting—meeting God, meeting people. Many
churches are paralyzed by a plethora of meetings, where
there is very little personal encounter of any kind, either
with God or with anyone else. Such a church is attractive
to very few inside and to nobody outside.

Open to Other Cultures

In laying such stress on releasing the distinctive gifts and
ideas of church members, so that the life of the church can
flow freely into its community, it is important to pinpoint
one final quality of openness. This, too, has its parallel in
Russian *glasnost*: being open and receptive to the richness
present in other countries and traditions. Paradoxically, a
church deepens its community life as it—at one and the
same time—turns unequivocally to the people in its neighborhood to become truly local *and* to the worldwide people
of God across the globe.

We will, of course, have to be selective about particular countries or ministries: one local church cannot be

constructively involved in the whole world. There is, however, immeasurable enrichment to be received from mutual interaction with Christians (and with people who are not Christians) in another country and culture. Traditionally, churches in the West have been giving and sending churches. It is now our turn—and long overdue—to be on the receiving end of God's riches in His people in Africa, Asia, and Latin America—and especially in the countries formerly in the USSR and Eastern Europe.

In our church in London, such partnership with the church in Uganda has brought untold challenges and blessings. Openness to *receive*—that is our need. To acknowledge that we are impoverished, shortsighted, spiritually undernourished, and poorly clothed. The world is now a global village—modern transport, which has opened up the distance between people living in the same local community, has also reduced the distance between people living on different continents. Are we open to these people?

PARRESIA

In concluding this overall perspective on *glasnost*, it will be valuable to establish the biblical rationale for making openness our essential priority in the community life of the local church. In the New Testament, in accounts of the activity of Jesus and in the developing life of the Church, one word occurs with striking regularity. The root word in Greek is *parresia*. It is used in John's Gospel to describe the openness of the relationship Jesus had with His Father in prayer, with His disciples in friendship, with the public in teaching. In the Acts of the Apostles and in the letters of Paul and John, it is a key word to describe the way the early Christians related to God in prayer, to one another in fellowship, to the public in proclaiming the gospel, and to their opponents when under pressure.

The origins of *parresia* are the political realities of

the Greek city-states in the fifth century BC—"the cradle of democracy." Democracy would never have got off the ground in cities like Athens, Corinth, or Sparta were it not for *parresia*. The word has the literal meaning of "saying everything" or freedom of speech: *the freedom to say what we believe or think without fear of reprisal.* It is an atmosphere as well as a policy, an attitude as much as a right enshrined in law.

The first followers of Jesus Christ, filled with the same Holy Spirit as their Master, began to operate in their community life in this atmosphere of *glasnost* and *parresia*. We are certainly not meant to follow any blueprint, from the Apostolic Age or from the success stories of today. We *are* meant to be open *with* God and *with* one another, open *to* God and *to* one another. This is the way to building true community life in the Spirit, as God recreates in local churches what Jesus Himself demonstrated in His daily life among us all those years ago.

Jean Vanier writes, "Community life isn't simply created by either spontaneity or laws. It needs a certain discipline and particular forms of nourishment."[2] This discipline and nourishment in a local church will be the subject matter of the rest of this book.

✻   ✻   ✻

1. What kind of church do we want (page 9)? In a small group of fellow Christians, brainstorm on this question and produce a "top-ten" list of desired ingredients for your local church.

2. What kind of church does God want? From the New Testament, identify God's "top-ten" goals for the church. Compare and contrast with your answers to the first question.

   This could be a long project if you want to do it thoroughly. Alternatively, you could read through one

book, such as Ephesians, writing down every goal for
the church that you can find.

3. Is your church characterized by thanksgiving? In what
ways? Why do you think that's so?

4. How much variety and diversity is there in your
church? What do you think about that?

5. How open is your church—to God? To outsiders? To
change? To risks? To one another?

6. Do you feel free to be yourself as a Christian in the life
of your church? Why, or why not?

CHAPTER TWO

LEADING THE OPEN COMMUNITY

I f there is to be *glasnost* in the church, those in leadership must set the pace, the tone, and the example. If leaders find themselves unable, for whatever reason, to be open to God and to the people, it will simply not be possible for a congregation to move far in openness. Because leadership is so crucial, we need at this point to uncover some of the most common obstacles in the path of such growth.

OBSTACLES TO OPENNESS

Omnicompetence

First, there are leaders taught and practiced in *omnicompetence*. Such people see any kind of weakness as something to be concealed, mainly because it is reckoned that people will be hindered in their faith and in their discipleship if leaders are seen to have feet of clay. Doubting—or indeed any loss or lack of certain faith—is seen as dereliction of Christian duty, as betraying God-given responsibility to set an example. If this attitude is maintained across the board, such leaders find it very difficult to cope with illness, for example, or with marriage difficulties—let alone breakdown. This approach to leadership cannot *afford* to be open: Its own convictions make vulnerability virtually impossible. Such people do not necessarily do everything themselves; they might be very much in favor of sharing

25

the work of ministry. But they see it very much in terms of giving tasks to others, not sharing themselves with others. They definitely hold the reins and keep everything in their control.

Doing Versus Being

A second obstacle to *glasnost* in the church is an emphasis on *doing rather than being*, on quantity not quality, on results rather than relationships. The pendulum has been swinging from such an emphasis in the last decade. Several trends have accelerated this. For example, the problem of burnout in the caring professions has attracted considerable attention. One main ingredient in burnout is drivenness, the inner compulsion to work long hours in the costly work of being available to people. This is usually accompanied by great feelings of guilt, if we cannot meet the needs and expectations of our people.

The realities of the "midlife crisis" have also been put plainly on the table, as people in their forties have begun to ask themselves what is the point of busy lives and what is being achieved anyway.

I think, for example, of one ordained leader who loves the work of Christian ministry so much that days off are difficult to enjoy and vacations are an intrusion. I myself was very similar in my approach to ministry when I was in my midthirties. I feel very differently now that I am in my early fifties. But it took an unexpected sabbatical year in my midforties to bring a different perspective.

At the same time the spiritual barrenness of busy lives has to come to the surface. In the greater honesty of today, Christian leaders have owned up to a loss of spiritual vitality and to drought in prayer. The shallowness of any one tradition of spirituality has led many to taste the streams of other traditions. Listening to God has become a theme to pursue by anyone in spiritual leadership, rather than the oddball preoccupation of a few unusual people.

Status-Seeking

Third, one of the most entrenched obstacles to openness is the matter of *status* in leadership. This problem has many sides. There was a time when the position of "pastor" or "rector" or "minister" carried its own clout. The person in charge was there because nobody else had the training and the theology required. Indeed, he was paid to do the job of running the church. If he ran it well, he would be well rewarded; if he did it poorly he would be shown the door—in spirit, if not in fact.

The expectations were clear on both sides and, with the expectations, there were also position, influence, and authority. The ordained person's role has gradually been pruned. Different professionals now take responsibility for several areas previously in the province of the clergyman— for example, the doctor, the psychiatrist, the social service worker, those in Christian education and music ministry, the administrator, the treasurer, and the fund-raiser. There is actually not much left for the ordained person to do. That is immensely threatening: Who am I and what am I here for?

The kind of training now available at many seminaries is often unhelpful, because it can concentrate on techniques for achieving success, programs that work, and other such matters, instead of on building vision for the kind of church God wants and an understanding of the kind of leadership God has selected to use. When insecure, status-oriented, and professionally fragile people find themselves leading churches full of strong, articulate, gifted Christians, it is very tempting to hide from honest, open encounter.

Past Experience

A fourth reason to run away from openness is readily understandable in the words "I tried it and they walked all over me; instead of responding in a similar vein, they used my openness against me and I felt completely betrayed." When this happens, as happen it does, it is not surprising that a person will be extremely reluctant to try again. It is costly and painful to be open in leadership; it will never be otherwise. When those in leadership set an example in openness, permission is given to others to be open—but opportunity is also given for others to manipulate and maneuver for their own ends. Because of this danger, it is important that we are committed, for strong personal and spiritual reasons, to pursuing an open style of leadership. Anything less than such a considered and consistent commitment will soon founder. By definition, openness means walking a road we have not traveled. The lure of familiar paths seems strong when we seem either to be going nowhere fast or, even worse, to be heading for dangerous rapids.

What are the characteristics of such open leadership? There are many, but let us look at four: shared leadership, servant leadership, accessible leadership, and enabling leadership. These are not watertight compartments, but it will be valuable to look at each in turn.

SHARED LEADERSHIP

Sharing Ourselves

We start with shared leadership because, after He had been commissioned by God, that is what Jesus began to practice. The gospels each make this plain in a distinctive fashion. Baptized in the Spirit, filled with the Spirit, Jesus saw Simon and Andrew by the Sea of Galilee and said to them, "Follow me." Leaders operating in the same Spirit will have the same approach. Jesus shared *Himself* with the men He drew to Him—not tasks or secrets or techniques or ideas, but Himself: "Follow me." Whenever He wanted to emphasize the nature of His Kingdom either to the inner group of disciples or to would-be disciples from the crowds, He would return time and time again to the simple but profound priority of following Him.

The most illuminating passage in the gospels for appreciating the way Jesus shared Himself with the Twelve is in the Apostle John's account of the Upper Room Discourse in chapters 13–17. Here we have the most complete and most intimate description of Jesus' relationship with the Twelve. He knew His time had come—the time for Him to leave them to carry on His work. It is often said that a person's ministry is properly seen in what is happening after he or she is gone. Jesus planned His strategy on the basis that His chosen disciples would carry on His work after He had gone, and that the work would grow and spread through them without His physical presence and example. This may turn out to be the most testing and searching criterion for our leadership: *If we choose not to share ourselves after the manner of Jesus with those around us, our work will wither and die when we are no longer on the scene.*

In chapter 13, John's first, comprehensive statement about the leadership of Jesus Christ is this: "Having loved his own who were in the world, he loved them to the end" (13:1). Love shares; those who love share themselves. Jesus loved the Twelve and in that love He held nothing back. He gave Himself to thèm; He gave Himself for them. John calls the Twelve around Jesus "his own"—the Greek phrase has the connotation of being special, personal, intimate, belonging, and owned, as if to say, "These men belong to Me; they are My responsibility and I acknowledge them as Mine. Although they live 'in the world' and are very much men of worldly passions and appetites, I have called them to belong to Me. They live in the world, but they are not of the world—'if you were of the world, the world would love its own'" (see 15:19). In this way Jesus emphasized the change of ownership and allegiance, in which He personally decided to take responsibility for the Twelve—"You did not choose me, but I chose you and appointed you that you should go and bear fruit" (15:16).

In the great High Priestly Prayer of Jesus to His Father

for His disciples in chapter 17, we see this special, personal, intimate relationship spelled out even more comprehensively. Here we see Jesus not simply talking of the Twelve as those whom He has chosen, but as those whom the Father has given to Him out of the world. He recognizes that they belonged to God before they ever belonged to Him (17:6). This fact has led Him to guard and keep them carefully throughout their three years of following Him. Jesus kept nothing back from them. He shared with them the words of God (17:8). He wanted them to know His joy (17:13), His glory (17:22,24), and His love (17:26).

In this astounding prayer we see why Jesus felt it important to explain to them, before He died, that He calls them "no longer . . . servants . . . but . . . friends" (15:15). The servant does not know what his master is doing, but friends are on intimate terms. So Jesus declares: "All that I have heard from my Father I have made known to you." It is not surprising that the disciples found the termination of such friendship traumatic and intolerable.

If chapters 13–17 of John's Gospel contained only such jewels, we would have been left with a moving account of a splendid friendship—and nothing more. The disciples (eleven of them by this time) would have struggled on in the wake of the crucifixion of Jesus (even taking into account His resurrection, His appearances to them, and His ascension into Heaven), reminding one another of their remarkable Friend and trying to carry on His work.

But, of course, the golden thread of these chapters is the promise of "another Counselor," a friend in like manner who would not merely be *with* them but *in* them, who would not stay for a short time only but would be with them forever, who would not do the preaching and the praying for them but would equip them to preach and to pray. In a sense, this Counselor would be their advocate and guide in a way Jesus Himself could never have been. They would know the same peace, the same power, the same persecution as He knew. His presence would be a deep-down experience. In all the pressures of living as friends and followers of Jesus, they would know an inner tranquility and a profound victory.

So Jesus continued with them, from Pentecost onward, by coming to be in them. He remained—and remains—the leader who shares Himself with His disciples, those whom He has chosen out of the world, but whom He recognizes to be a gift from God to Him.

Submitting to Christ

The reality of the Holy Spirit's work, in making Jesus real to His disciples and friends, is of crucial significance for shared Christian leadership today. First and foremost, Jesus Himself is the leader of His people, the head of His body, the great shepherd of the sheep, the One in charge and the One with whom the buck stops. It is imperative that we take this fact with total and practical seriousness. Whatever our approach to leadership, whatever our pattern of church government, *we must not push Jesus out of His proper place.*

If there is, therefore, one person who is the leader in a church, it continues to be Jesus Christ. If the buck stops anywhere, it stops with Jesus. If we look to anyone for final decision making, it is to Jesus. To take such an approach to leadership is not being ultrapietistic or unrealistic. On the contrary, it is to be serious and honest about the gift and the work of the Holy Spirit. It is to make practical sense of what it means to have within us and in our midst the unbroken and unending presence of Jesus. It is to practice the presence of God in our leadership.

This approach will mean taking time to listen to Jesus as head of His Church—and listening in stillness, without interposing any human insight or idea. Yes, we can and do mess up such listening to God with our own wisdom. But we must not allow our mistakes and our willfulness to dictate the way we operate. Faith in Jesus Christ as Lord means that, as leaders, we insist on listening to what He has to say to us. This listening will mean an open Bible as well as an open heart, an open mind and an open will. I fear that we actually sideline Jesus as Lord of the church by default, that is, simply by not habitually behaving as we ought with our Best Friend. To listen means to be still and to be quiet. It means not talking. Because God has given us two ears and one mouth, it means listening twice as much as talking. Jesus longs to speak to us, to share with us the words, the heart, the mind, the will, the plans of God.

It is exciting and stimulating to push back the boundaries in listening together to what God has to say to us. Every six months we spend as a staff team (eight or nine people) three days on retreat together. One major purpose is to spend quality time with one another and with the Lord. We have a lot of fun together. On one occasion, as we each shared in turn our feelings and fears, we spent time simply being quiet after each person had spelled out whatever he or she wanted to share.

This time of silent listening to the promptings of the Spirit took about fifteen minutes each time. When we eventually spoke what we had individually "heard" for that person, the pooled message was uncannily accurate and constructive—a combination of insights, scriptures, pictures, impressions, and exhortations. Jesus, through His Spirit, was clearly speaking to us.

Yes, we need to let Jesus share Himself with us as leader of His church. There are principles and patterns of leadership in His own three-year friendship with His chosen team that we can and should emulate. But the person traditionally or actually entrusted with leadership in any local church today is not to conclude that he or she is to play the role of Jesus in the team. This is a common trend in many churches. Too simple and straightforward a line is drawn from the model of Jesus' leadership to the model used by a pastor or rector.

For example, much is made of the way Jesus operated in His ministry of healing and deliverance. First, He did it Himself with the disciples watching; then He did it with them together; then they did it and He watched; finally He sent them out to get on with it. As a principle for learning on the job that is fine. What is often done with the model, however, is that the leader casts himself or herself as Jesus, and the others as disciples. When this experience of leadership becomes normal and determinative, it is not surprising to discover excessive trust placed *in* the leader and little peer group accountability practiced *by* the leader. Instead of stressing that he or she is as much a learner and disciple as everyone else, the leader gives the message from the outset that the others are to learn from him or her — and no amount of verbal insistence that "Jesus is the head of the church" can correct the warped expression of leadership that is already in place.

So, the person already entrusted with the traditional, formal responsibility for leading a church must learn from Jesus, but must not take over from Jesus. The work of God's Spirit within the person and within those whom God has given to that person will make possible the kind of sharing that was released in Jesus by the same Spirit of God. In the next chapter we will take a closer look at the practical details involved in shared leadership.

SERVANT LEADERSHIP

The Elusive Quality

The next characteristic of openness in leadership is being a *servant*. However commonplace and conventional servant leadership may be as a phrase, it remains elusive and unnerving as a way of life. Everything seems against it: our own natural inclinations, expressions of successful leadership in the world, expectations laid on leadership by congregations, specific examples of effective leadership in the Old Testament. Different countries and different cultures express patterns of leadership in anything but servant style. In Africa, tribal chiefs provide role models; in Latin America *machismo* rules; in the United States the cult of the charismatic individual dominates; in England the patron and the empire builder have still to be exorcised.

I will never forget time spent with a most impressive, humble bishop in Uganda — *both* for his example of servant-heart (shown in innumerable, costly acts of kindness to hundreds of visitors to his home), *and* for the shock of walking down the road with him to find women kneeling down in the dust in order to speak with him. I suppose we are living all the time with such contradictions (paradoxes is perhaps too self-justifying a word) — bishops who are enthroned and who also are called "my lord"; Christian leaders who expect large honoraria and first-class accommodation; churchmen who like titles and stand on status; disciples of Jesus who choose not to do menial work in church because "God has not called me to that." It is hard to think clearly in the midst of such a nonservant lifestyle. But it is possible to live differently. We can probably all think of those who, in the midst of immense authority and influence, still express the life and demeanor of a servant — but they are rare in any generation and culture.

Jesus' Lifestyle of Service
The obvious passage where we see servant leadership in operation is again in John's Gospel, chapter 13, when Jesus washes the disciples' feet. That was a servant's job. In a normal Jewish home on a Thursday night during Passover, the household servant would have provided this service to the guests. The upper room in that house in Jerusalem was, according to Mark's Gospel account, made available already prepared for Jesus and His friends (14:12-16). Presumably because any association with Jesus was dangerous by this stage, neither the householder nor his servants seem to

have been around at the time. Jesus and the Twelve had it to themselves. Who was going to be servant and wash feet? The indications in John's account suggest that Jesus waited to see if any of His friends might jump to it. Nobody did, so "Jesus . . . rose from supper, laid aside his garments, and girded himself with a towel. Then he poured water into a basin, and began to wash the disciples' feet" (13:2-5).

It is important to remind ourselves that Jesus did not merely adopt a servant's ministry at this particular moment and in this particular way. Washing His friends' feet was a particularly vivid and dramatic demonstration of doing the work of a servant—especially in such a context and in such circumstances. No, the whole of Jesus' life was lived from a servant's heart and in a servant's spirit. He did not simply do servant-like things at specific times; He "emptied himself, taking the *form* of a servant" (Philippians 2:7, emphasis added).

The Apostle Paul's classic description of Jesus in this passage portrays the preincarnate Christ as being "in the *form* of God." In other words, just as Jesus was in essence and in substance eternal God, so in His humanity He was in essence and in substance a servant. Whether the Greek word (in the language of both John and Paul)—*doulos*—has the nuance of slave or servant is hardly the point. Paul says that as a servant He emptied Himself. This word, which has been at the heart of theological debate about the nature(s) of Jesus Christ down through the centuries, has as its most down-to-earth meaning "he poured himself out," that is, emptied Himself in the way a bottle is emptied of its contents. Jesus did not hold Himself back, did not stint Himself, did not refuse to give away to others what He had received.

Furthermore, Paul's account mentions that Jesus "did not count equality with God a thing to be grasped." There were privileges and power attached to His eternal Godness. He did not hang on to these; He surrendered them; He left them behind . . . and never at any time in His humanness did He revert to these privileges. He was tempted to do so on frequent occasions. The most explicit was in Gethsemane on the brink of arrest and assassination. When the Apostle Peter drew a sword to fight the armed soldiers about to seize Jesus, He firmly told Peter to put away his sword—with the incisive words: "Do you think that I cannot appeal to my Father, and he will at once send me more than twelve legions of angels?" (Matthew 26:53).

Jesus never pulled rank. He never took refuge in status. He rejected any concept of hierarchy and taught His friends bluntly and uninhibitedly to do the same (Matthew 23:8-12). The titles and trappings of power were not for Him and His friends. For them and for Him the call was for servant leadership, that is, leading by serving. They called Him "Teacher" and "Lord"; they were right to do so. But, "If I then, your Lord and Teacher, have washed your feet, you also ought to wash one another's feet. For I have given you an example, that you also should do as I have done to you" (John 13:14-15). The word for example is *hypodeigma*, which means a pattern to trace carefully—that is, not an on-off action but a lifestyle.

I found myself recently in personal conversation with the cardinal archbishop of Westminster, Basil Hume. My own expectations of such an eminent leader in the Roman Catholic Church had been strongly geared toward titles and trappings, as in the world around us. The archbishop's manner and behavior were, in fact, utterly Christlike in his firm gentleness, complete lack of pretense or high-and-mighty airs, firm focus on the Lord, and readiness to do very humble things.

Humility
There is no doubt in the mind of Jesus that to become a servant requires humility—actually it requires humbling ourselves, which is something we do, not something we

wait for God to do in us. More than once He emphasizes that "whoever humbles himself will be exalted" (for
example, Matthew 23:12, 18:4; Luke 14:11, 18:14). In the key
Philippians passage, Paul asserts that Jesus "humbled himself." When Peter, the great self-asserter among the friends
of Jesus, learned the way of true greatness, he came around
to the same message—"Humble yourselves therefore under
the mighty hand of God" (1 Peter 5:6).

Jesus used one other motif in that same vein: "A servant is not greater than his master" (John 13:16, repeated
in 15:20). This phrase reminds us of Jesus' example, which
we are daily to trace. It is also a corrective to any easy or
overfamiliar attitude toward Jesus as anything but our Lord
and Master. The fact that He has come and lived among us
as our Servant enhances, not diminishes, His position as our
Master. We must never forget it. Instead, when Jesus uses
this aphorism in another context, He is content to leave us
with the following challenge: "It is enough for . . . the servant [to be] like his master" (Matthew 10:25)—a likeness that
will be demonstrated through a servant lifestyle and in an
encounter with persecution and slander.

ACCESSIBLE LEADERSHIP

Servant leadership will express itself in two particular ways:
it will be *accessible* leadership and it will be *enabling* leadership. First, it will be accessible and available. The servant
effectively makes himself or herself available to people. We
see this clearly in Jesus who is God-with-us. "The Lord is
at hand," writes Paul (Philippians 4:5). Jesus lived at Nazareth, walked around Galilee, stayed at Bethany, went up to
Jerusalem, passed through Samaria, visited Jericho. He was
here in our midst and all the time He was saying, by His
presence and by His actions, "I am here *for you.*"

This was true for the people of His time and place in
general terms. Jesus was there for them. In particular, He

was there for the poor—the blind, the lame, the deaf, the prostitute, and the tax collector. He was available to those in need of God. All that He had He had received from God for others. He was deliberately available to His disciples and spent that time sharing what He had with them—to the extent that He could remonstrate gently with Philip in the upper room around the supper table: "Have I been with you so long, and yet you do not know me, Philip?" (John 14:9). All those three years He had shown God to them and still Philip wanted to be shown God: "Lord, show us the Father, and we shall be satisfied" (14:8).

Taking Time to Be Alone
It is instructive to remind ourselves at this point that to be available and accessible to His disciples did not mean twenty-four hours a day every day. He habitually withdrew from them. He needed His personal space, especially to spend time in prayer and often to be refreshed. To be a servant, therefore, did not involve responding to the beck and call of even His closest friends. Yet we are probably right in saying that He withdrew from His friends as well as from the crowds precisely in order to be more available and accessible to them. In other words, He moved away in order to pray to His Father, but on behalf of others. The act—or rather the rhythm and the routine—of prayer was part of His servanthood. He knew—as we need to know—that He would more effectively serve others by safeguarding such times of personal renewal.

This principle is perfectly expressed in the story Mark tells about the disciples crossing the Sea of Galilee to Bethsaida. Jesus had made them get in the boat and make their way across the lake. The wind was in their faces and they were making extremely little headway. Jesus, in the meantime, had walked up into the hills to pray. The evangelist tells us that, from His vantage point above the water, "He saw that they were making headway painfully" (Mark 6:48).

So He decided to walk on the water to them. They naturally thought it was a ghost and were terrified. Then Mark says, "He got into the boat with them and the wind ceased" (6:51).

Jesus had needed to be alone with God. He was utterly exhausted by His efforts in feeding, both physically and spiritually, five thousand people. He moved away to pray so that He could move back with His disciples to serve them more effectively. So, accessible leadership involves a rhythm of prayer with God and availability to people. The leaders who are so swamped by people and their needs that they do not pray together, are not being servants to those people in any way that Jesus modeled.

Many leaders have found that they *must* plan their schedules carefully, in order to secure such a rhythm in a realistic way. We all start out with such priorities uppermost in our minds, but most of us let those gradually slide or become eroded. It is now over two years since such a rhythm began to reappear in my own schedule. I had allowed the traffic of human pastoral needs to invade my commitment to personal renewal on a regular basis. This invasion had happened, not all at once, but imperceptibly over the years.

It took a four-day silent retreat in an Anglican monastery for me to rediscover a different rhythm. That was hard enough. The next—and the more demanding—step was to establish such a rhythm back in the parish. That took over a year, and it was very much in fits and starts. In the end, it took a diagnosis of diabetes to force upon me what I had struggled to put in place during the previous twelve months.

Now, having firmly (with the crucial help of others close to me) determined what I should and should not be doing in ministry, I believe I have begun to get closer to a sensible, appropriate rhythm of prayer and availability.

Working as a Team
As we investigate further the implications of such accessibility and availability in leadership, it is worth stressing once

again the necessity of being in a team of leaders where this costly call of Christ can joyfully be pursued. The writer to the Hebrews delineates the responsibility on those in leadership as "keeping watch over your souls, as men who will have to give account" (13:17). Servants are always on the watch and available for whatever may be required. They are also accountable to their master for their actions. Such an awesome task is meant to be undertaken by a team, not by an individual privately. A team can be realistically available and accessible to a congregation; an individual cannot.

To take just one example, the Apostle James instructs sick members to call for the leaders of the church for prayer (5:14). No limit is put on their ministry. It is anyone who is sick, and their ministry is to be done regardless of whether the sickness is serious or not. There is no mention, incidentally, of such a ministry being a "homecall" ministry. If the leadership is present at worship, it makes sense for them to provide opportunities for the sick to receive prayer. This is an example of what it means to be accessible in a shared, servant leadership: "We are here for you."

If a team is going to be available and accessible to the congregation, they also need to be available and accessible to one another, particularly in giving and receiving ministry. This builds up the effectiveness, the experience, and the trust in a leadership team. They see God at work in their own common lives — and they develop confidence to be used in similar ways in their tasks among the congregation. They develop greater openness to God within them and through others.

In the leadership teams we have established in our church in London, this priority of availability has become uppermost after nine months of team life. When we first set up the teams, we knew we would have to be available to one another in personal support and ministry. Frankly, we have not succeeded in any significant way. We have recently been reassessing our life together as leadership teams, in order to find a pattern for our time together that genuinely builds on such mutual availability.

ENABLING LEADERSHIP

Power or People?

Finally, shared leadership will be resolutely and irretrievably intent on releasing the personal potential of others. A truly Christian leadership team will be enablers. They will see themselves as there for the congregation, not the congregation as there for the leadership. The life of a local church does not exist to provide a platform for certain people to share their gifts to fulfill themselves.

There is a strong temptation facing all those in leadership to use others for their own pleasure or to satisfy their own needs. The need to be needed is a common tendency among counselors. Preachers can use congregations to show off their own skills. Administrators can subordinate the actual needs of individuals to their personal desire to run a tidy system. Musicians and artists always have to watch the lure of producing a performance and looking for applause.

All these problems boil down to the same thing—are we wanting power over people, or do we want to see people blossom into what God wants them to become? In his letter to the Galatians, Paul urges the church not to use freedom in Christ as an opportunity "for the flesh," that is, to serve and indulge ourselves. Rather, says the apostle, "through love be servants of one another" (5:13). The love of God wants each person's very best. The love of God in us, especially in leadership, will make us sensitive to the gifts and potential of others. Paul went to the heart of it elsewhere: "Do nothing from selfishness or conceit, but in humility count others better than yourselves. Let each of you look not only to his own interests, but also to the interests of others" (Philippians 2:3-4). Only such an attitude will lead us to release others, rather than pushing ourselves forward.

I was struck recently, attending a conference in Birmingham, England, to hear something of the basic priorities underlying the leadership at Willow Creek Community Church in the suburbs of Chicago. The pastor, Bill Hybels, explained that all involved in any kind of leadership are held in an accountable fellowship, where the key question has become, "What is happening to your spirit?" In this way, leaders are being regularly challenged in terms of the way each is exercising his or her ministry—Is it in the Spirit or in the flesh? If it is perceived that a leader's spiritual life in not authentic, that person does not function as a leader until it is. This principle did not come across to me as in any sense heavy or judgmental—but healthy and vital.

A danger signal can be seen when we feel aggrieved when nobody appears to notice, let alone appreciate, all that we are doing for the church. We all need affirmation, but true Christian leadership is expressed in often-hidden work that sets others free to minister with their gifts. So enabling leadership does not dominate or hold on to the opportunities for ministry. It is looking constructively for ways others can develop and grow. It is prepared to stand down—to be stood down—in favor of another. The declaration in the annual Covenant Service of the Methodist Church becomes real when a person tells God he or she is willing "to be employed for Thee, or laid aside for Thee."

The priority of enabling leadership again brings to the fore our long-term goals. If we are with Christ in being determined to build *His* church, not ours, we will be looking far beyond our own period of leadership, beyond even our own lifetime. There is a certain pragmatism in this, as in every aspect of God's wisdom: by enabling others as widely and as fully as we can, we are actually building on the best possible foundation—that is, the special ministry of every member. Because it is plain from Paul's teaching on the Body of Christ (to switch metaphors from buildings to bodies) that every member/part of the Body has a crucial and distinctive role to play, we are stunting the growth of the Body unless we are enablers (1 Corinthians 12).

Perceiving a Person's Gifts

In most local churches there is more dissatisfaction due to underemployment than to overemployment. Gifts are lying stagnant or dormant. Individuals are not being stretched — or, if they are, it is the minority who are far too stretched. One of our biggest challenges in leadership is how to mobilize the membership. A basic prerequisite is to look for the potential ministry men and women possess. In the next chapter we will begin to look at this in more detail.

Jesus saw what a person could become. He saw that Simon could become Peter, and He never gave up on the man. He stood by him in all his petulance, pride, and presumptuousness. He refused to let him get away with his sins. He believed in Peter when Peter stopped believing in himself. He kept on breaking in on Peter's thinking and behavior, so that the man could not settle down into prejudice. He was ruthlessly firm with Peter, because to let him get away with such things could have both quenched Peter's potential and damaged the church of which he was a leader. Jesus was committed, in brief, to Peter's growth in maturity as a person and as a disciple.

The New Testament sparkles with examples of such enabling leadership. Barnabas could see in John Mark what Paul could never have seen. Paul realized that shy, sick Timothy could develop into an effective bishop of the church. Stephen was recognized by his fellow Christians as a man with outstanding leadership qualities, far beyond the practical ministry of organizing food distribution to the Hellenist widows. Ananias of Damascus could see what had happened to Saul of Tarsus and what might happen in the future, when everyone else, without exception, could see only a vicious persecutor of the Church. Priscilla and Aquila saw that Apollos had immense gifts as a teacher and so spent time instructing him in the way of God more accurately. The list is long and the need is urgent.

*   *   *

1. How would you evaluate the leadership in your church in terms of openness to God? Do any of the dissuaders mentioned at the start of this chapter operate in your church? (See pages 25-28.)

2. What do you understand by shared leadership? Do you agree that Jesus Himself must be the true Leader? How can that be worked out in practice?

3. What factors make servant leadership challenging and difficult in your church?

4. Discuss the proper rhythm in leadership of withdrawal to be alone with God and accessibility to the people in our care. What pressures can you identify that hinder such a rhythm?

5. To what extent can you detect any tendency in your church for leadership to become a platform for personal gifting and individual ambition?

CHAPTER THREE

TRAINING UP OTHERS

The story is told of a Swiss pastor on the verge of a breakdown who was urged to see the psychiatrist Carl Jung. When asked how many hours a day he was working, the pastor told Jung "about eighteen hours a day." Jung advised him to cut down to eight hours a day and spend the time thus released in quiet relaxation on his own. The pastor did this: the first day he sat down in a comfortable armchair to listen to Mozart and read a novel. The second day Mozart gave way to Beethoven . . . and so on. After two weeks or so the pastor felt, if anything, worse and returned to Jung, who asked him how, specifically, he was spending his time. When the pastor described his leisure hours, Jung said, "That is not what I meant; I want you to spend time quietly with yourself." The man replied, "I could not think of anything more appalling." Jung said, "Well, that is the person you have been inflicting on your people eighteen hours a day."

MOSES: HEADING FOR BURNOUT

Switch the pastor and Jung with Moses and Jethro and we see the same principle at work—the story is told in Exodus 18. The pressures of up-front, high-profile, virtually solo leadership had begun to tell on Moses. From Egypt across the Red Sea into the wilderness, past Rephidim and the Amalekites to Mount Sinai—it had been one long experience of pressure and stress, liberally sprinkled with miracles and triumphs. Jethro had "heard of all that God had done for Moses and for Israel his people." He recognized that "the Lord had brought Israel out of Egypt," but also knew something of the cost to Moses in this continuing lifestyle in the limelight, always under pressure to perform.

Neglecting His Family

Jethro was particularly sensitive to these strains and stresses because, as Moses' father-in-law, he had taken in Zipporah, Moses' wife, and their two sons, Gershom and Eliezer, when Moses earlier "sent her away" (18:2). We may only surmise what prompted Moses to send his wife back to her father's home with the two boys. It is likely that he reckoned that the work given to him by God as leader of the people was too dangerous and demanding for them; surely, he might have thought, they would be better out of the limelight and the pressures. Leaders think like this when they probably mean to say "*I* would be better off without you around me all the time." In a word, Moses did not want the extra hassle and responsibility of a wife and family. We may not, today, literally send our partner and children away — but we do so in every other sense.

Jethro listened sympathetically, but shrewdly, when Moses recounted "all that the Lord had done" while Zipporah and the boys were safely back home on the farm with Jethro. The wise old man also nodded sagely when Moses talked of "all the hardship that had come upon them in the way." He rejoiced with Moses "for all the good which the Lord had done to Israel." He gladly joined in the celebrations as Moses and Aaron prepared a feast for Jethro, Zipporah, Gershom, and Eliezer. The Lord had indeed proved His goodness and His greatness, but Jethro still had his own ideas about his son-in-law's priorities and lifestyle. He wanted to see for himself whether Moses was going about his leadership responsibilities in the most effective way. And he still harbored doubts about the wisdom of Moses choosing to ignore his responsibilities as a husband and father—however much he, Jethro, rejoiced in his role of grandfather. After all, *that* joy is rich precisely because you can hand the kids back when you have had enough of them!

Ignoring His Limits
The morning after the celebrations of the night before, Jethro was up early to keep a watch on his son-in-law's daily schedule. He was impressed by the younger man's sheer energy and availability. He could switch from one person's problems to another's in a moment. He managed a ten- or twelve-hour day without a break—it was people, people, people all the time. He saw everyone he could on his own—the others sorted out the crowds and gave their instructions. Some people stood around the whole day and had to go away disappointed. They were exhausted just waiting . . . and by the evening, Moses also was clearly worn out. Jethro was indeed impressed, but he also knew there had to be a better way.

He asked Moses, "What is this that you are doing for the people? Why do you sit alone, and all the people stand about you from morning till evening?" To Jethro's question Moses had the classic Christian activist's answer: "Because the people come to me to inquire of God; when they have a dispute, they come to me and I decide between a man and his neighbor, and I make them know the statutes of God and his decisions." The people want *me* to ask God what is right; they want *me* to make the decisions; they want *me* to interpret God's instructions to them; they want *me* to tell them what God has decided. I cannot opt out of my responsibilities.

Jethro, through the wise perspective of an older man and of an outsider, was uncompromising with Moses: "What you are doing is not good. You and the people with you will wear yourselves out, for the thing is too heavy for you; you are not able to perform it alone." What is the point of burning ourselves out, of imposing a driven, weary person on our people? The answer starts with the recognition that "*the thing is too heavy*" for one person, and it cannot be performed alone. The leader who refuses to listen to Jethro's wisdom at this point is doomed to burnout or breakdown. The Church of Jesus Christ is full of such examples. Once this simple fact is recognized and accepted, a better way becomes possible—and it is a way that actually reinforces Christian responsibility in leadership, rather than undermining it.

Learning to Rely on Others

Jethro emphasized that Moses should continue to "represent the people before God." He should "teach them the statutes and the decisions, and make them know the way in which they must walk and what they must do." So Moses should lead the people in prayer and teaching God's Word—but the major tasks of hearing people's problems and giving guidance about the ups and downs of daily life should be placed in the hands of others. These people should not be chosen irresponsibly nor only from an elite: they should be "able men from all the people, such as fear God, men who are trustworthy and who hate a bribe"—that is, gifted, godly, trustworthy, consistent individuals from every sector of the community.

Moses was called therefore not to relinquish his responsibilities, but to *delegate*. Not to throw the burden of leadership away, but to find others who "will bear the burden with you." He would still need to bring his wisdom to bear on any "great matter," which was either too complicated or too significant for those placed over "thousands . . . hundreds . . . fifties . . . tens."

It is doubly important that Jethro, in giving this counsel, offers it in a humble, nonaggressive, and nonjudgmental way. When challenged, Moses had firmly put Jethro in his place with God-talk. Jethro's response also mentions God, but in an utterly different tone and mood—"I will give you counsel and God be with you. . . . If you do this, and God so commands you. . . ." Jethro does not fall into the trap of meeting the pious pride of Moses with pious pontifications of his own. By his very demeanor and vocabulary he shows Moses another kind of leadership. The result is that Moses "gave heed to the voice of his father-in-law and did all that he had said."

Quite probably, Moses did not believe he could find enough people with the right qualities for this kind of leadership. Jethro had stressed, not expertise or professional qualifications, but personal character. Moses had a tendency to call the whole multitude a rabble of moaners and murmurers. Even without a pocket calculator, Moses would have realized he was looking for at least 130,000 individuals of the right caliber, if Jethro's counsel was to be heeded. But an essential part of Moses' greatness as a leader under God was his meekness (Numbers 12:3), and he recognized his own failures and the intrinsic authority of Jethro as the voice of God. So he radically, totally, and permanently changed his style and practice of leadership.

Moses redirected his ministry, even to the extent of keeping his wife and children alongside him from this stage on—only Jethro returned home, his job under God completed. If Moses changed because of Jethro, will Christian leadership today change because of Jesus? His approach to leadership, both in method and in content, was equally striking—and similar in pattern to that recommended by Jethro. There was a difference between the concerns of Jethro and Jesus: Jethro was addressing the *pastoral* aspects of God's work; Jesus was particularly involved in evangelistic ministry. Christian leadership entails both, and we can learn from both.

JESUS AND HIS TRAINEES

Jesus elected to work closely with the Twelve. They are described in the gospels in pairs—James and John, Peter and Andrew, Philip and Bartholomew, Matthew and Thomas, the other James and the other Simon, the two Judases. It is almost certain that Jesus instructed them, on their missionary ministry, to operate in pairs. Later he chose seventy-two others, whom the original Twelve presumably helped to train for their evangelistic work. If the original Twelve worked in pairs with these seventy-two, that meant that each pair worked with twelve. So the overall ratio among the Lord's own disciples, in terms of leaders to followers, was one to six—or better, two to twelve.

In our local church in central London we have recently adopted pastoral reorganization of a fairly radical nature. Over a period of six years the congregation grew to about six hundred. We had moved past the optimum number for effective working as the Body of Christ and the family of God—two metaphors for the church in the New Testament that carry the most important meaning for the organic life of a local church. We knew we had to recover both every-member ministry as the Body of Christ and personal, pastoral care for everyone in the family of God. There was a very strong temptation to press on with the momentum of growth by numbers, to retain a strong central pattern of leadership, to increase resources in terms of amenities and facilities, to add more specialist members of staff.

We decided, on the contrary, to divide the congregation into three distinct congregations, each with its own leadership team (mainly laypeople in normal employment) and each with its own worship service and network of home groups. Without having registered the precise mathematics operational under the post-Jethro Moses and later in the ministry of Jesus, I now realize that we in fact have one hundred in pastoral leadership of the total congregation—that is, one in six. Furthermore, the particular responsibilities of those one hundred people have been worked out in pairs—for example, leadership of home groups and specific portfolios within each leadership team. We asked for, held on for, trusted (and wavered in our trust) for the Lord's clear direction at an important period of church growth; we appear to have been led with precise care by the Lord. *But* we did not work out a structure in a mathematical or logical way; we tried to apply scriptural principles of leadership in the power of the Spirit, and we are only just beginning the new pattern of church life.

Certain things are clear after less than one year with this pattern. First and foremost, it *feels* right, and individuals have grown significantly through the stresses and strains of shared leadership, taking on greater spiritual responsibility than before, but also dealing with the nitty-gritty routine of running the life of a congregation.

It is also clear that it takes a lot of time and hassle to move from central, professional, and paid leadership to a more devolved pattern that mixes both full-time staff and busy laymen and laywomen. This is true in both directions: the clergy have to learn properly to consult and cooperate; the laity have to resist any temptation to let "the professionals" get on with it.

We have also discovered that such team leadership involves costly commitment to open expression of disagreement, as well as to perseverance in working through conflict. Such conflict comes partly from the sheer grating of personalities, but mainly from individuals who find they are being squeezed into roles, rather than being released into ministry appropriate to their giftings. More examples from our experience in recent months will come later in the chapter.

It cannot be adequately stressed how important it is to distinguish principles and dynamics from models and methods, whether in the Moses/Jethro encounter or in the ministry of Jesus and His first disciples. These principles and dynamics come out strongly in two seminal chapters in Luke's Gospel—chapters 9 and 10. These chapters describe the way Jesus imparted and implanted the open secrets of Kingdom ministry, first to the Twelve and then to the seventy-two. As we move into wider and more thorough training of potential leaders "from all the people," there is much to glean from what Jesus did and said in these two chapters. The parallel passages in Matthew (10:1-42 and 14:13-36) and Mark (6:7-13 and 30-56) are also relevant.

There are at least seven key issues addressed by Jesus in this training of the Twelve and the seventy-two. We'll look at them one by one in the rest of this chapter.

WALKING BY FAITH

First, Jesus expects and encourages them to *walk by faith* in their ministry. This ministry was "to preach the kingdom of God and to heal" (Luke 9:2). In both aspects they needed to operate by faith. They had little or no experience of either preaching or healing. Jesus promised a mixed reception wherever they went: so the faith factor would always be central, however many times they exercised their ministry. Before they set out, "he called the twelve together and gave them power and authority over all demons and to cure diseases"—a morale booster certainly, but they needed faith to put that authority to the test day by day, encounter by encounter.

This call to live by faith extended to their food, clothing, accommodation, and travel—no staff, no bag, no bread, no money; only the clothes they had on. He gave them no specific guidance about where to stay or whom to address; they were to find out which house and person was "worthy" (whatever that might mean) and act accordingly (Matthew 10:11-14). The Twelve had watched Jesus operate in this way; but watching was different from doing. Indeed, Jesus seemed to expect them to do the kind of healings He was doing, cleansing lepers and even raising the dead (Matthew 10:8). They also had to overcome their all too natural fear of the violent and crude forces of evil within people ("demons"), in order to stand up to these forces and by faith expel with a word—as Jesus had done.

None of these actions would have come easily or naturally to the disciples, whether the Twelve or the seventy-two, nor did Jesus pander to their feelings of inadequacy and fear. To both groups He said, "Behold, I send you out as sheep in the midst of wolves" (Matthew 10:16 and Luke 10:3, where the seventy-two are called "lambs" rather than sheep)—hardly a commission calculated to inspire confidence in their ability to succeed. And yet, it was, in a strange way, a stimulus to faith in God, as distinct from confidence in themselves, to be made fully aware from the outset of the sheer impossibility of their mission in human terms.

One main discovery we have made, as a result of our pastoral reorganization into three distinct congregations, is that the best things happen when we truly are helpless and hopeless. A group of young married couples, for example, felt motivated to start a special outreach service for people with young children in the neighborhood. They began, however, with a mothers-and-children activity on a Wednesday morning. It was a daunting experience that became more daunting when the Sunday half-hour service was started several months later.

But as a result a young woman has been converted, setting off what portends to be a chain reaction in her family. Several new families have come to try out the Sunday service, which is run entirely by laypeople new to leadership. They have felt very raw and green. They have tasted the impossibility, humanly speaking, of the situation. But they have taken two or three steps of faith, and God is honoring them.

Much modern training for leadership in the church seems to be focused on producing people equipped and qualified to get results. People may feel inadequate when initially launched into leadership, but so many techniques, programs, resources, and ideas have been fed in that the "lambs in the midst of wolves" experience is one from which many seem to be insulated or anesthetized.

Because authentic ministry is so impossible in human terms, it is vital to keep in place the principles of *shared leadership* and of *working in pairs*. The actual encouragement and incentive of working together inspires faith, especially where a person acting alone could be tempted either to show sheer bravado or to run a mile. Two are certainly better than one in the ministry of the Kingdom.

Today we need to reinterpret what it means to walk by faith in Christian leadership, given the fact that in most local churches we are not in a position to start from scratch like the Twelve and the seventy-two. However, it is important to remember that all churches face a pagan, ignorant (about Jesus), at times hostile, local community. Usually it is unevangelized, and fresh, bold initiatives are required to fulfill our mandate to go and preach, cast out demons, and heal.

Perhaps the right priority is to go out two by two in such situations, deliberately putting to one side any method or resource that is not consistent with the Lord's instructions to His disciples in these chapters. We might do this just once in our local situation simply as an experiment, to see what happens if we give ourselves to such a vulnerable ministry of preaching, casting out demons, and healing the sick, going "blind" into the situation in the faith that the Holy Spirit will direct our feet, our minds, our mouths, and our hands. The Twelve responded to the Lord's commission as follows: "So they went out and preached that men should repent. And they cast out many demons, and anointed with oil many that were sick and healed them" (Mark 6:12-13).

It is certainly true that disciples grow best and learn fastest when thrown into the deep end. Time and time again I have seen individuals respond to challenges they (and often I) never thought they could face. Invariably their "saving grace" has been the fact that they have been working in a team, accountable to and supported by one another. Far bigger steps of faith are possible when we are all in it together. Equally, it is easier to risk one's reputation, health, composure, or life when working in pairs.

COPING WITH EXHAUSTION

The second issue Jesus faced with His disciples was how to *cope with exhaustion* (Luke 9:10-17). There is a fascinating point and counterpoint in this sequence of events. When the Twelve returned from the pressures and the exhilaration of their evangelistic travels, Jesus "took them and withdrew apart" (Luke 9:10). Mark's account is fuller and more explicit: "The apostles returned to Jesus, and told him all that they had done and taught. And he said to them, 'Come away by yourselves to a lonely place, and rest awhile.' For many were coming and going, and they had no leisure even to eat. And they went away in the boat to a lonely place by themselves" (Mark 6:30-32).

The apostles had been on the go for many days, teaching and healing, traveling from village to village and from town to town. They had slept in different beds virtually every night. They had been emotionally and spiritually drained. They had seen results of varying kinds—from dramatic deliverance from demonic bondage to fierce opposition from people who rejected them and all they stood for. Their adrenaline was still flowing as they returned to Jesus and debriefed with Him. Jesus knew what they did not know—that they needed rest to recharge their batteries and to be alone with Him.

But then the problems began. "Now many saw them going, and knew them, and they ran there on foot from all the towns, and got there ahead of them" (Mark 6:33).

Jesus has a striking reaction to this invasion of their privacy and desire for quiet renewal. He had compassion on the crowds, whereas the Twelve became increasingly filled with frustration and resentment. Jesus saw the crowds to be "like sheep without a shepherd," harassed and helpless. So He set about the ministry of the Kingdom: "He welcomed them and spoke to them of the kingdom of God, and cured those who had need of healing" (Luke 9:11).

The disciples, by contrast, resented the crowds and wanted to be rid of them. In the evocative phrase of Luke, "the day began to wear away." At last, they thought, Jesus will send them away—"to lodge and get provisions" at least, and probably they won't bother to come back in the morning. Jesus had raised their expectations of a good break away from the people: it was now all the more difficult to go on being ministers of healing and deliverance.

"You give them something to eat." With these abrupt and ridiculous words Jesus brought them face to face with a fundamental truth about the Christian ministry: *service to the Kingdom of God requires the strength to cope with exhaustion.* Yes, they needed to establish a rhythm of work and prayer, of ministry and rest. But they also had to be flexible enough to be available to people when that was right. Jesus Himself deliberately withdrew from people on a regular basis. He also made a point of doing so at decisive moments in His life. Here, however, He impressed on His disciples that compassion can overcome exhaustion. The sheer impossibility of providing food for five thousand men, "besides women and children," forced them once again toward an act of faith. Jesus took the initiative, established what human resources were available, organized the crowds for efficient distribution, prayed to His Father in Heaven, called on the cooperation of the Twelve—and people were satisfied.

By this action, Jesus helped the disciples see that "they who wait for the LORD shall renew their strength, they shall mount up with wings like eagles, they shall run and not be weary, they shall walk and not faint" (Isaiah 40:31). He had Himself amazed them by His ability to keep going without normal rations of food and rest. He told them, "I have food to eat of which you do not know. . . . My food is to do the will of him who sent me, and to accomplish his work" (John 4:32,34).

In practical terms, we will probably find it necessary to take time out with exhausted leaders, at reasonably regular intervals, to evaluate honestly the factors that have brought them to this point. I recently heard of a church where leadership of home fellowship groups was a commitment people are expected to take on for life. I could hardly believe my ears. Quite apart from many other crucial considerations, such an approach virtually guarantees exhaustion, if not collapse and breakdown.

Evaluation (we do this once a year, and most leaders commit themselves only for twelve or eighteen months at a time) helps each leader to weigh his or her commitments to the church's ministry in relation to other commitments. We should be encouraging one another to take sabbaticals from regular leadership. We should also be encouraging one another, when our commitments have been assessed and endorsed, to hang in there when exhausted until it is right to take a break.

One particular couple have struggled on, amid a welter of growing responsibilities at work and in the church, and I for one ought to have seen clearly that their exhaustion was not the passing result of a particularly busy period in their lives, but the inevitable sequel to mixing and matching two incompatible arenas of responsibility in the church.

In Christian leadership exhaustion comes often, not from doing the work God has given us to do, but from doing work God has *not* given us to do. Jesus made it plain (and this comes in the same context as these chapters on training the disciples) that the yoke He places on our shoulders is easy and His burden is light (Matthew 11:30). When we are genuinely involved in God's work, our capacity is supernaturally stretched and we surprise ourselves with our resilience and resources. When our "Christian" work, on the other hand, is self-inspired or imposed upon us, we often feel permanently worn out—it is all such a burden.

So, Jesus was instructing His disciples in a vital ingredient of Christian ministry—*learning to distinguish the call of God from the call of our own desires and needs*. Within that lesson came the distinction between, on the one hand, proper rest in the rhythm of work and worship and, on the other hand, getting worn down and worn out by pressures and expectations that come from someone other than God Himself.

When training others to take up Christian leadership, we need to help them absorb this lesson. After many years of pressuring people to take responsibility in the local church, I realize that there are at least two questions those contemplating leadership need to ask themselves: "Is this a responsibility to which *God* is calling me?" and "Is this a responsibility to which God is calling me *now*?" When putting such tasks before people, we need to give them all the time and space they need to become as convinced as possible about these two matters. There are few things more fraught with hassles than Christians in leadership who do not feel that God wants them there at this, or at any, stage.

FACING FAILURE

The third issue Jesus addressed in training His disciples was the need to *face up to failure*. This emerges from the events on, and at the bottom of, the Mount of Transfiguration (Luke 9:28-43 and Mark 9:2-29). On the mountaintop, three disciples saw the glory of Jesus; at the foot of the mountain, nine disciples tasted their own helplessness and failure. Three saw into Heaven; nine wilted before the powers of hell in a demonized child. Three had a mountaintop experience of blessing; nine realized how useless they were—even though not so long before they had seen demons bow to the authority of Jesus in them on their first evangelistic foray into the countryside.

It is not surprising that, soon after this experience of failure (coupled with the special blessings given to Peter, James, and John on top of the mountain), "an argument arose among them as to which of them was the greatest" — an argument that led to Jesus addressing a fourth issue, with which we will deal in a moment. Failure is invariably linked with the success of others and with our own previous successes, both of which accentuate the failure we now experience.

What Is Success?

There are several perspectives on failure in the accounts of this incident in the gospels. First, the disciples needed to come to terms with what constitutes "success" in the Kingdom of God. The matter in hand is a demonized child who is convulsed and shattered when the demon seizes him (Luke 9:38-39). As we have already noted, the disciples had only just returned from traveling through several towns and villages, during which time many demons had been cast out of individuals. They must have seen this ministry as extremely successful.

Indeed, when the seventy-two returned from a similar period of ministry, they were over the moon about their dramatic success: "Lord, even the demons are subject to us in your name!" (Luke 10:17). There are few experiences in Christian work more exhilarating than seeing demons leave people and submit to the authority of the name of Jesus. It is extremely tempting to draw out this ministry, to engage in protracted conversations with demons, to revel in our authority to walk all over "the power of the enemy" (Luke 10:19). Jesus gave such authority to the Twelve, to the seventy-two, and to His Church. *But* He told the seventy-two unequivocally, "Nevertheless, do not rejoice in this, that the spirits are subject to you; but rejoice that your names are written in heaven" (Luke 10:20).

Jesus clearly wanted to reinterpret "success" for His disciples. It is all too easy to take on board worldly criteria of success — and casting out loads of demons is certainly one criterion the world's achievers would recognize, at least if someone in their family was the one set free from the powers of darkness. By contrast, Jesus urged the disciples to rejoice that their names were written in Heaven. That is, they were to rejoice in what God had done for them, because they cannot write their own names in Heaven; in what holds good whatever may or may not happen in their work and ministry; in what is true into eternity in the fullness of God's Kingdom, not what happens in a given moment in time, but can then be forgotten or overtaken by very different events.

This lesson remains paramount for all involved in Christian leadership. We are called by God to be His fellow workers, to hold lightly to what the world terms success, to press ahead with what God gives us to do, and to count neither the cost nor the "notches on the gun." Our joy is in being redeemed children of the living God. So, the nine disciples at the foot of the mountain could rejoice in the midst of their failure with the demonized child, *in spite of* this failure. Their names had not been blotted out of the "Lamb's book of life" because they had failed to cast out a demon. Their eternal salvation and their acceptance with God were not dependent on success or failure in ministry, but on the work God had sent Jesus to accomplish by His death. That is why Jesus immediately stressed that He was going to be killed . . . and raised to life again (Mark 9:30-32).

I have found that any week of ministry is full of failure, usually prosaic and not all that public. I fail to carve out time to pray, to pastor, to prepare properly. I meet with several people who seem to get nowhere with me and I get nowhere with them: I fail them. I fail to cherish and nourish my wife. I fail as a father. I fail to do the things I ought to do — a phone call here, a visit there, a letter, a word of encouragement or correction. There are the more sizable and substantial failures, too. Unless I believed deeply that I am accepted by God on the basis of the work of Jesus, not my work, I would go around the bend.

Expect Failure
Linked with this part of the lesson about failure is the simple truth that Christian ministry is *not* one continuous story of blessing and success. Many modern biographies and stories of the work of God suggest — or even assert — that it is. The book market is saturated with such accounts, and such books have extremely strong appeal — they certainly enjoy the biggest sales. In the short period described in the gospel accounts at this stage, the nine disciples went from casting out demons to being unable to cast out demons. Jesus had given them authority "over all demons" (Luke 9:1). So why could they not deal with this particular demon? There is clearly nothing automatic in being God's fellow workers — we can assume nothing and we should presume nothing. We are not God, therefore we cannot and should not play God. Jesus is the Head of the church, and He determines when, where, and how. He knows that it is good, indeed necessary, for us to taste failure. It reminds us that we are "of the earth, earthy."

Learn from Failure
But there is more to failure than simply tasting it. We need also to appreciate more thoroughly the reasons for failure. These Jesus addressed with the nine disciples, who had by that time been joined by Peter, James, and John. If we compare the accounts of the incident by Matthew, Mark, and Luke, we discover important and intriguing lessons. The chief lesson is about faith, faithlessness, believing, and unbelief. When Jesus is presented with the situation, He expresses His own frustration with that "faithless generation": "How

long am I to be with you? How long am I to bear with you?" The child's father pleads with Jesus to help them—"If you can do anything. . . ." Jesus replies: "If you can! All things are possible to him who believes." The father then utters the classic cry of the desperate seeker: "I believe; help my unbelief!" Jesus responds to this mustard-seed faith with deliverance and healing for the child.

Matthew's account of the aftermath (17:19-21) reveals that the disciples asked Jesus "privately" why they could not cast out the demon. Jesus unequivocally explains: "Because of your little faith." In that He then states that faith the size of "a grain of mustard seed" can move mountains, He obviously reckoned the faith of the disciples to have been minimal, if not invisible. We have, then, the perspective that a desperate father has more faith—though by his own admission not all that much—than the nine disciples of Jesus with a recent track record of success in casting out demons. This has to be an essential ingredient in training Christian leaders to face up to failure: *The humblest, most wobbly seeker will often outstrip them in demonstrating the qualities God is looking for in His Kingdom—and notably in exercising faith.* More than that, we can become too sophisticated by far in defining faith. The father was desperate, and in his desperation he believed. The disciples were, initially, confident, and in their growing desperation stopped believing.

In Mark's account a different lesson is emphasized as Jesus faces the disciples with their failure: "This kind cannot be driven out by anything but prayer and fasting." Some manuscripts omit the fasting, but prayer-with-fasting is prayer that means business with God, rather than with food and drink as distractions, so we can safely assume that such fervent prayer is intended by Jesus in such a situation. Now, prayer is intimately and inextricably linked with faith—if we do not pray or are not praying in a given situation, we are placing our faith in ourselves, not in God. It is in prayer that we express our faith in God. The Christian leader who does not pray will — immediately, soon, or eventually — fail. It is imperative, then, that we face up to failure and, in particular, to the prayerlessness that produced it.

We do not know whether the nine disciples at the foot of the mountain prayed about the demonized child — it is likely that they did not. They did not have the most congenial circumstances in which to work. The scribes had mingled with the crowds, and it looks very much like a put-up job — with the child a prize exhibit to support the detractors of Jesus and His disciples. Whatever the build-up and the nature of the encounter, Jesus indicates that "this kind" of demonization requires prayer with fasting. In other words, there are demons and there are demons. In certain more stubborn cases, concentrated, continuous prayer is necessary, or demons will not leave the person.

It is difficult to determine what Jesus intended to convey by "this kind" of demon. Its particular characteristics are described in some detail in Mark's account: it manifested itself in the boy only spasmodically, seizing him and dashing him down, causing him to foam at the mouth, grind his teeth, roll around on the ground, and become rigid. On several occasions the demon cast the boy into the fire and into water in attempts to destroy him. This appalling scenario had been present from childhood. The father described the demon as "a dumb spirit" but, when Jesus addressed it, He rebuked it with the words "you deaf and dumb spirit." One assumes that Jesus identified the spirit more precisely than the father, thus articulating His complete authority over it. Jesus knew what to do and Jesus also knew what He was dealing with — a deaf *and* dumb spirit, a demoniac, not an epileptic (the gospel writers are clear about the difference — Matthew 4:24).

How did Jesus know these things? Because He had been in prayer. Luke tells us that He took the three disciples up the mountain "to pray" (Luke 9:28), and He was in prayer — and fasting — for twenty-four hours or so. He was able, in the power of the Spirit, to cast out this kind of demon. Interestingly, the three disciples were "heavy with sleep" (Luke 9:32) while Jesus prayed—as they would be later in the Garden of Gethsemane—and they were in no better state to cast out this kind of demon than the other nine. So the realities of failure had to be faced, in fact, by all twelve. They had received from Jesus authority over *all* demons: this demon had refused to budge.

Take Risks
In some arenas of leadership, failure in the realm of the demonic is unknown—not because people always succeed, but because the demonic dimension is either denied or avoided. The facts of evangelistic ministry in the 1990s in all parts of the world require that we all take proper account of the demonic. It is all too easy to go to extremes, to see demons everywhere and in everyone. It is also all too easy to evade an essential part of our Lord's commission by pretending there are no such things as demons. This is particularly irresponsible in a generation up to its eyes in occult and supernatural practices—certainly in as rife and pervasive a way as in first-century Palestine.

COMPETITIVENESS

The fourth issue Jesus tackled with His disciples was *competitiveness*. We have already remarked on the inevitable contrast between the three up the mountain and the nine down the mountain. Peter, James, and John were regularly selected by Jesus to be present on particular occasions. There is no explicit reason for this special treatment, although we can with hindsight recognize the distinctive ministries given to each of the three after Pentecost. None of the other nine had such a high profile. This itself could have led to envy and competitiveness.

We know that Mrs. Zebedee, mother of James and John,

held very high ambitions for her two sons—and she was totally uninhibited in coming to Jesus to ask for them the two top places in the Kingdom of God (Matthew 20:20-21). Debates about who was the greatest among the disciples and in the Kingdom were, apparently, frequent. We have clear statements to this effect in the gospels. We also have regular teaching from Jesus about the priority of humility, and about His own example of service. In addition we have the emphasis, in His own practical ministry, on those whom contemporary society effectively ignored or even directly oppressed.

We can also be sure that the first-century disciples of Jesus were no different from the disciples of Jesus today. Modern disciples have one eye on what their fellows are doing, thinking, receiving—and they do not want to be left out. Peter was speaking for every disciple, then and now, when he erupted at the way Jesus did not merely allow, but even seemed to compel, the rich young ruler to turn away from discipleship. Having watched this splendid candidate for their rather motley group leave Jesus in sorrow, Peter exploded: "Lo, we have left everything and followed you. What then shall we have?" (Matthew 19:27).

In the way Jesus responded to such outbursts and to arguments about precedence among the disciples, he regularly turned popular thinking upside down. He used language like "the first shall be last," "the least shall be the greatest," and referred to children and servants. Such teaching was calculated to expunge normal human thinking from the minds of the disciples.

Our recent decision to become three congregations in the one parish church has underlined vividly the dangers of a wrong spirit of competitiveness. We have struggled with this among the three clergy involved. We have wrestled with it in the three leadership teams. It has surfaced frequently among members of the three congregations. Plenty of people have been ready to compare congregation with congregation. The Corinthian syndrome ("I am of Paul, I am of Apollos, I am of Cephas") has threatened to disrupt our life together on several occasions.

We are not out of the woods yet. Probably we never will be, and to expect that we will is unhelpful and unrealistic. We *have* discovered, however, that such competitiveness must be named and confronted in the power of God's Spirit.

If team leadership is going to work in a local church, it is necessary to train all involved in such radical ideas about precedence and greatness. The competitive spirit, in which virtually everyone is schooled from a very young age, needs to be identified, addressed, and renounced. It will not disappear quickly or easily; indeed, it will keep on emerging. Paul was the supreme competitor and high achiever. He realized that nothing less than the inner dynamite of God's great love within him could set him free from such competitiveness.

The love of God constrains us to bring our gifts into Christian leadership, not in order to excel over others, but in order to build up the Body of Christ in a spirit of service. This is Paul's emphasis in 1 Corinthians 12, when he uses the metaphor of the human body to explain how mutual cooperation is natural to the different members of the body—if they did begin to compete with one another, the body would soon be in a mess. Each part needs the other parts—and is all too aware of it. In another letter, Paul reaches the point of urging the Christians to "count others better than yourselves" (Philippians 2:3), rather than doing anything from selfishness or conceit.

Team sports are an excellent way of distinguishing the individualist from the cooperator. An individualist might make one or two brilliant moves, but he or she still needs to dovetail with the rest of the team. It is accepted that a team of less talented people will always triumph over a collection of talented individuals. Individuals do not always have to be individualists.

So it should be with those working together in the ministry of God's Kingdom. Jesus wants us all to bring our very best to His Kingdom, to *be* the very best we can be—but not to do so in a spirit of competitiveness with our fellow Christians. It is important to discern how the different gifts in a leadership team complement one another, to be sensitive to the best way any one person is drawn out and the conditions under which each one begins to feel threatened or discouraged. Another key is learning genuinely to affirm, not just a person's gifts, but the person himself or herself.

This becomes particularly significant when anyone is unable to make a contribution, perhaps because of illness or other pressures. At times like this we all need to know that we are loved whether we can perform or contribute or not. It is interesting to note how many people feel useless and discarded when they finish an office or a task. Someone else takes their place and they return to relative obscurity. No longer in the limelight, they feel ignored and rejected, even if the initiative to withdraw from leadership came voluntarily in the first place.

Clearly, none of these issues in ministry can be dealt with by doing a course at a seminary or a spell of lay training. These are classical "on the job" training issues. We learn as we do the work with others in a team that is mutually accountable and supportive. We go on learning until God's Kingdom comes in its fullness.

RECOGNIZING SECTARIANISM

So far we have looked at walking by faith, coping with exhaustion, facing up to failure, and dealing with competitiveness. The fifth issue is *recognizing sectarianism.*

Inclusive or Exclusive
This rears its head not long after the incident with the demonized boy at the foot of the mountain. The fuller account comes in Mark 9:38-41:

John said to [Jesus], "Teacher, we saw a man casting out demons in your name, and we forbade him,
because he was not following us." But Jesus said, "Do
not forbid him; for no one who does a mighty work
in my name will be able soon after to speak evil of
me. For he that is not against us is for us. For truly,
I say to you, whoever gives you a cup of water to
drink because you bear the name of Christ, will by
no means lose his reward."

In Luke's account John's opening remark is in answer
to what Jesus had just said; that is, anyone who receives a
child in His name was actually receiving Him, Jesus. A child
was least and last in contemporary Jewish society: giving a
warm welcome to the least and last was to give a warm welcome to Jesus — and such a welcome was, in fact, to welcome
"him who sent me," that is, God the Father.

The key phrase that links these two incidents is "in my
name." Jesus is explaining to His disciples what it means
both to bear His name and to invoke His name. They bear
His name and are learning to live like those who bear His
name. Such people will do certain things and show certain
distinguishing marks. For example, they will be open and
warm with children. They will challenge demonic forces.
They will be generous with those in need, even in need of
the simplest things like a cup of water.

In other words, those who bear the name of Jesus will be
particularly committed to people who are normally shunned
or ignored; they will be firmly opposed to evil, however it
manifests itself, and will be used by the Spirit of God to do
mighty works in releasing people from the grip of the Devil.
They will do little, unseen, unspectacular things wherever
they find someone in need. They will also speak highly
of Jesus.

These evidences of true discipleship are in tension with
John's forbidding the man to cast out demons, "because he

was not following us." We presume that this incident took place when the apostles had been sent out two by two on their evangelistic mission. Jesus' teaching now forced John to reappraise his own attitude and behavior. This is still one major function of our Lord's teaching, but it can be done with effectiveness only in the kind of learning situation described here—that is, on the job.

John wanted to draw a tight circle around the Twelve and stop anyone from getting in. Jesus, in effect, wanted to remove the boundaries and was prepared to accept anyone not opposed to Him: "He who is not against us is for us." John's attitude was exclusive and Jesus' was inclusive. The two attitudes reflect two different approaches to membership of the Church of God, attitudes reflected in church life today. Some denominations and church groupings draw firm and tight boundaries for membership; others have virtually no boundaries, even going beyond Jesus' instructions that we need to be living and operating in His name. When that prerequisite is ignored and a person's attitude to Jesus is regarded as unimportant, liberalism has gone too far. Equally, the way Jesus dealt with John in this passage challenges our exclusiveness.

Such exclusiveness is close to sectarianism. Sectarianism is the attitude that maintains that one's particular emphases and convictions are right, and anyone who does not follow them is wrong. A sect is convinced that it alone has the truth. A Christian church is committed to Jesus alone as Truth. It is fully consistent to hold the second position and to have an inclusive, welcoming, and open attitude; to be ready to listen and to discuss; to accept people into the general life and interaction of the local church; to make allowances for the gaps, blind spots, question marks, and contradictions in the understanding of fringers, seekers, and agnostics. To become "a church without walls" is a risky experience, but it is preferable to becoming a watertight bastion of orthodoxy without any way of access.

Overprotecting the Truth

A sectarian spirit is subtly pervasive. For instance, John no doubt thought he was being properly protective of the name and reputation of Jesus. After all, Jesus had given authority over demons only to the Twelve: So what was this lone ranger doing casting out demons in the name of Jesus? A similarly overprotective, proprietary attitude can easily infiltrate Christian leaders. Some are threatened when they see unauthorized people taking the initiative unilaterally, without consulting those with more experience. Even making allowances for proper lines of authority in the church, it is essential to encourage disciples to act on their own initiative. We live in the day of the entrepreneur, and they need room to move. If those in leadership hold everything tightly and insist on central control, they stifle the life of the Spirit among the people of God.

It is this kind of exclusiveness that causes bottlenecks in the free flow of spiritual life in a church. One essential characteristic of true Christian leadership is a commitment to encouraging and releasing the gifts of everyone in the church. This, as we have seen, involves seeing leadership in terms of availability to others, so that they can be enabled to contribute. This principle holds good in every facet of local church life—preachers look to train and liberate preachers; evangelists encourage emerging evangelists; those entrusted with leading the music ministry create opportunities for others to express their gifts in a creative way; counselors take note of those with gifts in counseling; administrators delegate tasks for others to perform; those skilled in Christian education invest their skills in those who can teach others. Any suggestion that only we have what it takes needs to be eliminated.

Interchurch Cooperation

The same principle applies to a local church's relationships with other Christian churches in the neighborhood.

We are enriched by mutual interaction and partnership. One significant fact of life in Christian ministry is that the ordained professionals lay less emphasis on the priority of interchurch cooperation than church members do. Also, a visiting preacher, especially one who comes from a different background and tradition from the resident pastor, invariably seems to receive a more positive response than "the home team." The message may be almost identical, the delivery not so polished, the style less arresting—but a new voice works wonders.

Exposure to Other Cultures
Even more important, in checking tendencies toward sectarianism, is regular openness and exposure to the church of Jesus Christ in other cultures and countries. The church in the West is particularly inbred and narrow-minded at this point. The most incisive, enriching, and challenging perspectives on discipleship are available from Christians in Africa, Asia, and the countries of Eastern Europe formerly under communist control. Modern communications and travel give us little excuse for burying ourselves in our little exclusive world.

John was protecting his own position under the guise of protecting the reputation and the ministry of Jesus. Jesus had one word for him—"Don't." He wanted His disciples to start out with the same openness with which He Himself had come to us. Paul was equally clear: "Welcome one another, therefore, as Christ has welcomed you, for the glory of God" (Romans 15:7).

Gathering or Scattering
If down the track it becomes apparent that an individual is not gathering but scattering, then we must recognize that such a person is against Jesus—even if the person says he or she is with Jesus (Luke 11:23). This complementary saying of Jesus comes again in the context of casting out demons—in

a strange way such direct encounters with demons force the issue of a person's true allegiance: Is he or she for Jesus or against Jesus?

The reference to gathering and scattering is most significant in the context of the unity of the church, particularly the need to avoid any sectarianism. Both words, *gather* and *scatter*, are used to describe what happens to sheep (John 10:12-16). The Good Shepherd gathers the sheep from different folds to become one flock; the hireling scatters the sheep. Those called to share in pastoral oversight of the flock of God are bound, therefore, to ask themselves whether they are gathering or scattering.

GETTING RID OF PREJUDICE

The sixth issue on Jesus' training agenda is *getting rid of prejudice*. Again it is John, along with his brother James, who reveals the secret attitude lurking in the hearts of the disciples. Jesus had passed the point of no return in pursuing His God-given mission: "When the days drew near for him to be received up, he set his face to go to Jerusalem." The cross was His focus from this point onward. He was experiencing the cross in His inner being—He wanted His disciples to see and absorb the significance of the cross. He was not prepared to let anything or anyone divert Him from the way of the cross. He was also not prepared to allow any personal prejudice to blind the disciples to the purpose of His death on the cross.

Savior of the World
John and James had such a personal prejudice. On His way from Galilee to Jerusalem, Jesus deliberately chose to travel by way of Samaria, even though historically Jews and Samaritans never ate at the same table (John 4:9). Jesus had already done this journey going in the other direction, from Judea to Galilee. On that occasion His encounter with the

married woman of Sychar led to the conversion of many Samaritans (John 4:39-41), who declared, "We know that this is indeed the Savior of the world" (John 4:42).

John is the only gospel writer to record that incident. We know that his prejudice against the Samaritans received a severe roasting in a later encounter. As Luke tells the story, the villagers on this occasion refused hospitality to Jesus—"because his face was set toward Jerusalem" (9:53). John's reaction—and that of his brother—was immediate and fierce: "Lord, do you want us to bid fire come down from heaven and consume them?" They saw themselves in the role of Elijah, who had acted in the same way with messengers of the king of Samaria many centuries before (2 Kings 1:9-16). Samaritans cannot change their spots, thought the brothers; they worshiped Baal then, they probably worship Baal now on their own special mountain; they loathe Jews and despise our mountain of Zion; now they have insulted the true King of the Jews; let's get God to punish them.

The response of Jesus is fascinating, especially if we accept the fuller version of certain manuscripts—"He turned and rebuked them and he said: 'You do not know what manner of spirit you are of; for the Son of Man came not to destroy men's lives, but to save them.'" From John's blatantly racist remarks Jesus bluntly disassociates Himself. Whatever Elijah may have done, Jesus is the Mediator of a completely new covenant between God and the world. Under the Old Covenant, of which Elijah was the most zealous guardian, racial purity was of the essence. Jesus, the Son of Man, had come to bring salvation to the whole world, irrespective of race, culture, and historical feuds. The Samaritans in Sychar had cottoned on to this glorious truth: "This is indeed the Savior of the world"—Jew, Samaritan, and Gentile. To draw any other conclusion, let alone revert to blatant racism, is to be inspired by a spirit totally opposed to the Holy Spirit of God.

It is imperative, amid all the ghastly feuds of the twentieth century, that those called into Christian leadership are in the vanguard of rebuking all manifestations of racial, cultural, religious, or historic prejudice. All prejudice spawns violence. The world today is riddled with such violent feuding. Christians, as disciples of Christ, must not take sides, but rather insist on proclaiming in Christ full and free salvation for all, irrespective of any human criterion, and that the church is open to all.

The Cost of Rejecting Prejudice

Such a Christlike stand will be costly. For example, we surely need to challenge, in the name of Christ, any version of the gospel that suggests Jews have more rights before God than Arabs. Similarly, the religious bigotry in Ulster on both Protestant and Catholic sides of the divide should be renounced and rebuked in favor of one true church centered and founded on Jesus Christ. Tribal allegiance in countries like South Africa and Uganda are to be surrendered in the face of Christ's call in this story to His disciples to reject violent reprisal.

What becomes increasingly clear is that discipleship bites in a civil-war situation. That was the situation in first-century Palestine, and it is widely prevalent in the world today. Most of the world's publicized trouble spots are civil-war situations: for example, Ulster, South Africa, the republics of the former Soviet Union, Yugoslavia, Peru, Cambodia, Zaire—these are the places in the headlines as I write. Americans probably know as well as anyone that civil wars leave scars that last for decades, if not centuries. Nothing but the cross of Christ can bring true, deep, lasting reconciliation when brother's blood has been shed by brother on local streets and in familiar fields.

It is in this profound sense that the Church of Jesus Christ is the hope of the world. It is not surprising, therefore, that John is so summarily and stringently taken to task by

Jesus. Such prejudice is anathema to Him, and must also be to His disciples. Because it is so insidious and pervasive, the only effective way to tackle it is in the partnership and fellowship involved in on-the-job training.

FOLLOWING WITH SINGLE-MINDEDNESS

The seventh matter Jesus tackled with the disciples was *following with single-mindedness.* It is easy for single-mindedness to develop into a hard, unattractive, proud, remote kind of zeal. Indeed, each of the previous six issues of discipleship can be lost on people who are single-minded in the wrong way. Such people develop a hard attitude toward those with whom they disagree; tend to write off anyone who is not as single-minded; become highly competitive and measure everything by results; are unable to recognize failure and certainly cannot cope with it; never own up to exhaustion but always go at everything hammer and tongs; have their lives organized and their plans so clearly laid down that prayer and faith easily go by default. If this is a caricature, it is still sufficiently recognizable to make us careful to discover a proper single-mindedness.

In the relevant passage (Luke 9:57-62), Jesus tackles the issue in the light of three encounters on the road. As each took place in the company of the disciples, Jesus took the opportunity to shed a little more light on what it means to follow Him. The actual word, *follow,* comes up in all three conversations. It is central to the call of the apostles, and it vividly describes what it means to be a disciple of Jesus. Whatever else it might mean or not mean, being single-minded means keeping our eyes on Him and walking in His footsteps (see 1 Peter 2:21).

The Apostle Peter knew only too well that as disciples of Jesus we can follow in His footsteps or at a distance. When Peter followed at a distance, he denied he ever knew Jesus (Matthew 26:58,69-75). So careful, close following is essential.

Following a Lord on the Move

The first encounter, according to Matthew (8:19), was with a scribe who came up to Jesus with an unconditional declaration of intent: "I will follow you wherever you go." Even if this scribe had not listened carefully or often to Jesus, even if he had not yet appreciated that following Jesus would take him to the cross, the man's heart was clearly in the right place. The scribes, as a group, were hostile to Jesus. By this stage in the Lord's public ministry, their opposition to Him was being orchestrated. Jesus had recently told His disciples, though not the crowds, that He would be rejected by the elders, chief priests, and scribes (Luke 9:22). A number of scribes had conducted a public argument with the nine disciples at the foot of the mountain over the case of the demonized boy (Mark 9:14).

It could well be, of course, that this scribe had started by arguing with the nine disciples, but had been so startled by the way Jesus had delivered the boy and healed him, that he had a complete inner revolution—deciding that this Jesus was indeed the Son of Man written about in the book of Daniel (7:13-14). As a scribe, the man would have spent weeks in the book of Daniel in his theological studies. He would have recognized that Jesus of Nazareth actually could be the figure prophetically described in that strange book—"to him was given dominion and glory and kingdom, that all peoples, nations, and languages should serve him." The scribe wanted to serve this all-conquering Son of Man: "I will follow you wherever you go."

It is significant that Jesus did not turn away, but spelled out with precision the lifestyle He, as the Son of Man, would consistently adopt on the road to claiming His Kingdom with the words "Foxes have holes, and birds of the air have their nests; but the Son of man has nowhere to lay his head." Jewish contemporaries of Jesus, especially those versed in the scriptures of the Old Testament, saw the Son of Man as a triumphant hero, living in style and sharing the spoils of victory with His followers. Jesus disabused the scribe of any such ideas — He wanted no disillusioned followers then, and He still does not want them. Decisions to follow Jesus must be based on a realistic understanding of His mission and ministry. To follow Jesus is to join and share in that ministry. In one very important sense, foxes and birds have a more secure existence than the followers of Jesus. He was always on the move — ready to go on to the next place at His Father's instructions. The followers of Jesus can never settle down or feel they can rest on their laurels.

This, then, is Christian leadership and Christian ministry. We learn it on the road with Jesus and with one another. We discover the growing sense of freedom of being in a worldly sense insecure. We don't know what comes next, where the Lord is going to go next. In offering to follow Him wherever He goes, we are signing away our own freedom to choose what is involved in ministry and leadership. If He says "Come with me into this situation," we cannot refuse. We are committed to Him and to our fellow disciples. We cannot afford to put down permanent roots, but we are to be ready to up and leave when He says so. His dominion, power, and Kingdom extend universally, but they do not necessarily include material prosperity or worldly success.

Following Jesus First
In the second encounter, according to Luke, Jesus takes the initiative: "To another he said, 'Follow me'" (9:59). Jesus moved into this man's life just as He had with Simon, Andrew, James, and John. He issued an invitation and a challenge. All five of these men had seen adequate evidence on which to base a decision. Jesus had — in their presence — healed, taught, and delivered people from demons. Now He came to them and said, "Follow me." The man He addressed had pressing family business: "Lord, let me first go and bury my father."

In the Middle East the dead were buried within twenty-four hours — there were no refrigeration facilities and inquests were unknown. Deaths happened nearer to home. This man had heard of his father's death only within the past few hours, and it would take him a few more hours to bury him with the appropriate respect and dignity. It was the natural, decent, accepted, and acceptable thing to do, and only an unreasonable, uncompassionate person would think otherwise. But Jesus said to the man: "Leave the dead to bury their own dead; but as for you, go and proclaim the kingdom of God."

The key to understanding this story is that Jesus Himself approached the man and took the initiative in calling him. If Jesus thinks that now is the time and I am the person, then He must come first. The man said, "Let me first . . ." — and that was where he failed to be single-minded. He had other things (a funeral) and other people (his father) on his mind. Jesus knew about funerals and fathers, but He specifically chose to call the man at that particular moment in time. He knew what He was doing and He knew the problems He was causing, but He was concerned for the Kingdom of God and He saw the man as essential to proclaiming that Kingdom. When Jesus decides to call a person to such a ministry, everything else and everyone else pales into relative insignificance. Nothing else can come first.

That devastating phrase, "Leave the dead to bury their own dead," places the call of Jesus in another sharp perspective. All who are not disciples of Jesus are dead — "dead through trespasses and sins," according to the Apostle Paul (Ephesians 2:1). If we allow ourselves to get submerged by death and the dying, we will never respond to the call of Jesus. We are surrounded by death — "In the midst of life we are in death." A dead world needs people committed to proclaiming the Kingdom of God. That means single-mindedness, especially in the harsh, sad realities of death.

It is tempting to be bland and banal under the guise of

being sensitive and compassionate in such circumstances. The man could, in fact, have proclaimed the Kingdom of God to his family by the very act of leaving them to follow Jesus. That particular moment in the experience of a family is often the time for empty words and gestures, observance of form and familiarities, rather than facing up to reality. The father was dead but life must continue. Jesus was inviting the son to begin a new life, life in the Kingdom of God, life following Jesus. His family might have criticized him, but they would not have failed to appreciate the importance of deciding what place Jesus was to have in their lives.

Following Without Conditions

The third person in these little cameos of discipleship comes to Jesus with a mixed decision: "I will follow you, Lord; but let me first say farewell to those at my home" (Luke 9:61). The man wanted to follow Jesus and made that clear in his approach, but he had already worked out a condition on which he would follow Him. The previous man had reacted to the initiative of Jesus with another priority in his life. This man had weighed the call to discipleship and added a proviso—his relationships at home had to come first.

This man stands in Scripture for all who attach their own conditions to Christian discipleship. We all have such conditions—explicit or implicit. Single-mindedness means unconditional discipleship. It means trusting Jesus with our relationships at home, recognizing the possibility that "a man's foes will be those of his own household" (Matthew 10:36). It means taking on board the deeper truth that our real brothers and sisters are the disciples of Jesus Christ, "those who hear the word of God and do it" (Luke 8:21). It means taking seriously the perspective that those related to us in the family of God through the blood of His Son are closer to us than our blood relations.

Of course, the condition(s) we often attach to discipleship may concentrate on other needs and desires—for example, I will follow You if You heal my illness, give me a marriage partner, sort out my work situation, guarantee me a certain lifestyle. All these private agendas are made public in this third encounter. It is in the nature of on-the-job training that all such private agendas can be exposed. If this is what discipleship is all about, then training for leadership in the Kingdom of God must bring them out in the open.

These, then, are the issues Jesus tackled with His disciples, among many others. He was training them to take on His work and ministry, to be servant-leaders in His church. Unless we make a priority of these matters, we will not be producing Christian leadership worthy of the Name.

1. Are there signs of burnout in your local church leader(s)? What do you see?

2. What is the difference between true delegation and merely handing over particular tasks?

3. If you were to follow Jethro's principles of deploying the gifts in your church, how many would you be looking for to take on pastoral responsibility?

4. Consider the seven issues Jesus addressed in His on-the-job training of the disciples, and spell out what each one would mean in your situation. What needs to be done to bring these on the agenda of your local church?

5. Identify the potential leaders in your church, with whom such an agenda of discipleship-training could be pursued.

CHAPTER FOUR

KEEPING IT SMALL

T he first three chapters have spelled out what a local church looks and feels like, when at its heart is Christian community as lived, taught, and imparted by Jesus, the Lord and Head of the Church. We have concentrated on qualities and priorities in leadership, with a particular emphasis on learning from the way Jesus trained His disciples for leadership as service and in holy living. A local church committed to such Christian community, and moving ahead in the priorities and power of the Lord, will be characterized by openness to God, to one another, to the local community, to the world, to the future.

In the next seven chapters we will be looking at several aspects of such local church life in more practical, specific ways. We begin with a fundamental, nonnegotiable priority: small groups. This subject is, at one and the same time, filled with the greatest potential for exciting growth and fraught with the greatest panic about disintegration. Pastors and ministers everywhere have struggled with small groups. We have seen new life blossom and flourish like springtime, only to be killed off by frosty relationships or bugs in the system. Yet we all know instinctively and biblically that small groups simply have to be and have to work. Jesus operated with a small group. The apostolic churches consisted of small groups meeting in homes. Virtually every major revival or past outbreak of spiritual life down the centuries has been expressed in, if not actually inspired by, small gatherings of believers—whether in the monastic tradition or in more evangelical Protestant circles (to take simply two opposites in the spectrum).

What, then, can be said about the healthy growth of such small groups as the warp and woof of local church life? In this chapter I want to be very practical and realistic, drawing on experience both from the churches I have served and many more with which I have been in contact, either through personal visits or through private correspondence. I am convinced that, unless we get on the right track with small groups—and do so in the right spirit and on firm theological principles—we will short-circuit most of what could happen in a church.

Most of the situations in which I have been involved, directly or indirectly, have progressed over the years from small groups as one of several options for church members and their friends, to home groups as the essential foundation for discipleship in its fullest sense. Most local churches will be in a similar position. How do we move from the one situation to the other? If, in a voluntary society such as a local church, people have been used to groups where attendance was optional and spasmodic, in which participation was limited in scope and intention, how can we help people to see something richer and more meaningful? Where does any sense of imperative come from, especially a *divine* imperative? The beginning of an answer lies in developing a vision for such home groups.

A VISION FOR HOME GROUPS

Here are two statements about the purpose and vision of such groups. The first comes from a church in Cape Town, South Africa, that began to move in this arena in 1974 and is reflected in a leaflet made available to the leadership of twenty-four groups in the congregation in 1990. It reflects a growing understanding of and commitment to what they have designated "house churches," thus emphasizing the all-round nature of these groups:

> House churches are small home-based communities drawn from and linked to the larger church (i.e. the local congregation), dedicated to the service and worship of God. . . . House churches need to be geared for personal, corporate and numerical growth, not merely maintaining equilibrium. . . . House churches aim to encourage and equip their members to live their lives as authentic disciples of Christ. . . . House churches should foster a secure environment which encourages the risks necessary for growth in discipleship.

The second statement comes from a church near Liverpool in northwest England. For some time this church had worked with "households of faith," but they wanted to move into a more comprehensive and outward-looking pattern of group life. In 1987 they adopted a title, "neighborhood home groups." Three years later, they had twenty-one such groups, to which about half the congregation was committed. In a leaflet given to every person in the congregation, the question is first asked: "What is a neighborhood home group?" To which the following answer is given:

> A neighborhood home group is a small Christian community which has its life centred upon a particular home in a neighbourhood of the parish of Upton, or in an area outside the parish boundaries. It is usually composed of about twelve believers who live near to one another. . . . The members of a home group meet together at least once every two weeks. They give a high priority to attending these meetings, but belonging to a home group is not just a matter

of attending certain meetings. It is rather a matter of
participating together in the Christian life of a small
community of believers, to whom we are committed
in a particular way. Living near to one another makes
it easier to put this community life into practice.

The leaflet goes on to spell out a bit more what this will
produce:

> Belonging to a small Christian community, in which
> one can know people well and be well known by
> them, gives a particular opportunity to put into
> practice "the new commandment" of Jesus to his dis-
> ciples: "Love one another as I have loved you." As a
> part of loving one another in this way, we seek to help
> each other to understand, to be encouraged by, and
> to apply the teaching of the Bible in our individual
> lives and in our life together. . . . In a house group we
> have the opportunity in the neighbourhood where we
> live, not just individually but together as members of
> the body of Christ, to reach out to others with the love
> of our Lord, both by responding to people's practical
> needs and by telling people the good news about
> Jesus. . . . In a house group every member of the
> church has the opportunity to discover and use their
> gifts in the Lord's service.

When we are introducing such house groups to potential leaders in our congregation in central London, we find
it important to explain two aspects of the vision: the *features*
of a healthy group and the need for a *life cycle* in each group.
Let me explain these two aspects.

Five features characterize a healthy home group: pastoral care (so that members find it a place of safety and a
point of accountability), Bible study, worship, evangelism,
and "lots of fun." To find a proper balance of these features

is an essential part of effective leadership. We will look at these ingredients in a moment.

The need for a life cycle is equally important. Like the aforementioned characteristics, it emphasizes that such groups, like a local church, enjoy organic life rather than organized activities. We have discovered that there are six stages in the life cycle of a home group: conception and gestation, birth, growth, marriage and procreation, maturity, death. Later we will look more thoroughly at each stage, but recognizing the reality of these stages helps leaders and members to hold true to a vision for their life together.

Before going any further, let us look at both aspects of the vision. We return to a phrase in the Cape Town leaflet: "small home-based communities drawn from and linked to the larger church." Over the years this factor has proved fundamental for healthy growth. Home groups that live to themselves die by themselves amid much frustration, recrimination, and aggravation. It is biblically right for home groups, if they are to be the warp and woof of discipleship in a local church, to be linked pastorally with the church's life and leadership. This means, also, developing pastoral networking between leaders of different home groups, so that there emerges a strong sense of partnership in ministry. Otherwise, each home group gets isolated and oscillates between independence and introspectiveness.

It will become increasingly obvious that bringing such house groups into being and providing appropriate nurture is a major priority. So let us look more thoroughly at a home group's life cycle.

THE LIFE CYCLE OF A GROUP

Conception and Gestation

The first stage is conception and gestation. A lot needs to happen behind the scenes and by way of preparation before a group sees the light of day. The local church as a whole must get used to the idea and catch hold of the vision. This takes time. It may well be that only a few are prepared for such new life in the family of God, prepared for the changes and the cost involved. Good time will be spent on selecting and training suitable leaders. Much prayer is necessary to ease the process of gestation and to help people accept the realities of what is happening. This process cannot be rushed. It will more likely begin with only two or three such home groups in a congregation: in Cape Town in 1974 it was two.

When it becomes clear who does want to be involved, much care and prayer needs to go into the selection of people for groups. It must first be decided on what basis such choices are to be made. For example, the principle of neighborhood has much to commend it if a home group is to be truly effective in reaching out.

Another principle that has to be addressed is, Who decides who goes into which group? In many churches a process of natural selection prevails; that is, friends invite friends. This has both advantages and disadvantages. Home groups that are called into life and added to on this basis can become very protective and exclusive, as well as being rather homogeneous. They will find a common life easier to establish than others, but they may find the life of God's Spirit more elusive — or they could assume that *bonhomie* and *camaraderie* in a Christian *milieu* necessarily mean spiritual growth.

The time of gestation will also cause not a few anxieties and fears to surface. For example, the absence of suitable leadership will tempt us to abort an embryonic home group. It is, perhaps, important to remind ourselves that, in certain circumstances, birth is premature but the baby still survives. All births are precarious, and there is no such thing as a hazard-free creation of home groups. Because the life of a home group does provide so much necessary nurture for the people of God, we can often trust a number of Christians to get on with it—redoubling our prayers, but also believing that God can look after what He Himself has quickened into life. It is always good to tell ourselves that, whatever we do in planting and watering, God is the One who gives the increase (1 Corinthians 3:7).

Birth

The moment of birth is always memorable, usually anticipated with great expectancy, a privilege if we can participate in it, full of hopes and fears. The first gathering of a house group has all of these dynamics. Sometimes it is fairly straightforward: no complications, nothing special or striking. Some groups get off to a dramatic start with weighty needs being shared and the challenge to mutual support on the table from the word go. Others can be slow to get going, rather ponderous and a bit depressing for keen committed leaders.

However the birth of a home group takes place, it is just the beginning of something that will take a long time to find its feet. Much Christian work founders on the reefs of high human expectations. Some people invest too much in the success of a home group, especially if they have waited a long time to join one. We must always place our hopes and expectations in God, not in human beings. Every member needs to have a strong commitment to make it work, and to do everything possible to bring that about.

For all these reasons, it makes sense if the opening meeting of a home group is kept very informal, is not packed with too much, provides time and space for people to chat (over a meal), involves a fun exercise that helps people learn a bit about each other, has one clear spiritual ingredient, and is not allowed to go on too long. The old adage still holds good that you stop while the people still want more. If the birth is protracted, it takes longer to kindle enthusiasm about its ongoing life.

Growth

In the Cape Town church already mentioned, each member of the congregation is told clearly what the task of a "house church" is — "growing disciples." The invitation is "to journey along with others in our Christian growth." House churches "provide caring, supportive and stimulating environments where you have the opportunity to grow in your faith along with other Christians."

In the briefing given to leaders it is clearly stated that "house church membership involves commitment to explore the Christian faith, and desire to grow in love and in the knowledge of the saving Christ and in submission to his Lordship."

This growth is given a threefold dimension in the same leadership leaflet — "House churches need to be geared for personal, corporate and numerical growth, not merely sustaining equilibrium." Tension soon becomes apparent in any house church or home group when some people are resistant to growth in any dimension — personal, corporate, or numerical. All of us at certain stages in our lives — perhaps when we are worn out or facing trauma at home or at work — find the realities of growth too painful and too costly. We want to coast, not climb.

But growth is essential to Christian discipleship. If a child does not grow, we know there is something seriously wrong. In the Cape Town example, growth was expected in discipleship, in faith, in love, in knowledge of Christ, in submission to His lordship. As individuals experience growth in these ways, so the group as a whole will move toward the kind of corporate growth God intends. Equally, as the group grows in its life together, so this will rub off on individual members. There is a two-way ministry here.

Now, it takes time for evidence of real growth to become apparent. It is, therefore, unreasonable and unhelpful to be looking frequently for obvious signs of growth in the group. The other church mentioned earlier, near Liverpool, actually unites in an annual review of the whole life of each group in the light of its stated goals:

> We consider prayerfully how we have sought to put these aims into practice over the past year, and we seek the Lord's leading as to how we can more effectively put them into practice in the coming months. At this time each member of the community also considers prayerfully whether they think it is right for them to continue as a member of this home group or whether the Lord seems to be leading them in some other direction.

In our London church, where the rate of change and the mobility of the congregation is probably greater than the church near Liverpool, we actually require only a year's commitment to a home group (all things being equal), because we find it necessary to reorganize the home-group network each September. Leadership of a group, therefore, is taken on only for a year. Growth may happen faster in such a hothouse, but it is also likely to be less steady.

Another valuable means of evaluating growth is through a central leadership meeting on a regular basis—perhaps every four to six weeks. This can meet several needs: training of leaders on the job, mutual support and encouragement, information from and discussion with the central leadership of the church, assessment of how each group is going.

As the sheer number of groups in a congregation grows, it becomes important to develop pastoral care for leaders in manageable numbers, probably one experienced person looking after the leadership of three or four home groups. Otherwise the central staff will become swamped, and the pastoral care of leaders, which is so crucial for steady growth, will go by the board. Most churches with more than four or five home groups develop a system of shared pastoral care.

Numerical growth is one main aim of a home group.

Jesus entrusted His Church with the commission to go and make disciples; part of what it means to grow in discipleship is to make other disciples. A growing disciple is a maker of disciples. So the authentic growth in Christ of a home group will cause others to join the church. It may well be that, after initial contact with and conversion through the home group, new disciples are better grounded in another group, which is specially geared and specially designed. Then they can return to the home group in which and through which they found faith in Jesus as Lord.

Marriage and Procreation
What we will realize, hopefully sooner rather than later, is that such effective growth will require a home group to consider multiplication. We call this part of the life cycle *marriage and procreation*. It is good to recognize this stage and to be constructively anticipating it early in the group's life. If we wait until it is upon us, we will find it much more difficult to encourage people to leave in order to start life in a new group.

There are many ways this multiplication can take place. A group can simply divide two or three ways—each part forming the nucleus of the new groups. Alternatively, the group may specifically choose to send out two or three members to form, in consultation with the central church leadership, a new group. Two or three from one group could combine with two or three from another to form a third, thereby creating space for change in their former groups.

I remember one group that was so teeming with life and leadership potential that, when the time came for forming several new groups in the church, this group provided leadership for at least four others. Clearly, this particular group had worked hard on recognizing and releasing people into active responsibility within the group. Such spotting of leadership potential is part of the essential life of any group. One regular task of pastors is to sound out home-group leaders about potential leaders. We find that it is necessary, indeed vital, to have training in place for potential leaders regularly throughout the year. Such courses along with on-the-job training, which home groups provide by their very life, provide a steady stream of new leaders. There is still, I hasten to add, a shortage of leadership.

Maturity

All these stages in the life of home groups—conception, gestation, birth, growth, marriage, and procreation—lead disciples on to maturity. Maturity is not a place we reach and can then say that we have arrived spiritually, either as individuals or as a group. The Apostle Paul makes this very plain when he urges those who are mature to follow his personal example of habitually forgetting what lies behind and continually straining forward to what lies ahead (Philippians 3:13-15)—that is, to nothing less than the prize of the upward call of God in Christ Jesus. The mature disciple, then, is one who knows he or she is not mature and looks for more.

In the life of a home group, this expectant straining forward to become all that, in Christ Jesus, we can be will come out in several ways. It will be noticeable that people care for one another, that they are open and truthful, that there is a high level of trust, that decisions are made by consensus, that there is a strong team-commitment to the group, that conflict is faced up to and worked through, that people listen carefully and properly to one another, that people are free to express feelings as well as convictions. There are other signs of true Christian maturity, but a home group worth the name will know something of these realities.

Death

Although the Church of Jesus Christ is eternal and cannot be conquered or destroyed by death, any particular manifestation or local expression of it here on earth is provisional and will have to die. This is particularly true of a home group—of all home groups. Part of its maturity is its willingness to die and its acceptance of its moment of dying. This will come about for any number of reasons—perhaps something so obvious as several members moving away from the area.

It could, on the other hand, be a rather more radical and disruptive reason. When we realized God was calling our church in London to stop being one congregation (with two services of worship and a single network of home groups) and become three congregations, each with its own service and network of groups, we faced an extremely painful fact. We needed to bring all the existing home groups face to face with certain death, in order that new life might spring up in each of the three congregations. So every home group had to die. There was an element of encouragement in the mere fact that everyone faced the same bereavement.

Tertullian, an early Church Father, said, "Our people die well." Sadly, the history of the church shows that we are not nearly so good when it comes to facing the demise of those outward forms in which we have come to discover and express the life of Jesus. A former archbishop of Cape Town, Bill Burnett used to say that the church needs a lot of planned death in order to release resurrection-life. He was thinking of particular ways that the church has expressed its community life. The old saying—"a man, a movement, a mission, a monument"—all too accurately sums up the situation, not least in the structures, organizations, and groupings in a local church. If home groups are to be different from such organized systems in churches, one of the best things they can do is to learn to die at the right time. It is, after all, only Christians who believe that death precedes life and that the name of the game is resurrection.

ESSENTIAL FEATURES OF HOME GROUPS

Let us now return to the essential features of home groups. The Cape Town leaflet mentioned six—teaching, worship, prayer, developing gifts, witnessing, and sharing. In London we stress five—pastoral care, Bible study, worship, evangelism, and "lots of fun." The church near Liverpool has a good summary—looking upward, looking inward, looking outward. Let us take these three now.

Looking Upward

"At the heart of our life together is our recognition of the presence of the risen Lord Jesus among us and our worship, by the Spirit, of God our Father and Jesus our Lord. We are a community of celebration, rejoicing in the Lord our God and seeking to give him the thanks and praise of which he alone is worthy." There are many dimensions to worship, and in chapter 5 we will take a longer look at them. At this stage it is important to recognize that home groups have distinctive opportunities, as well as specific limitations, when it comes to being communities of joy, celebration, praise, and thanksgiving.

The major limitation—that is, the expectation we bring from the larger congregation of what it means to worship God, or rather what we think we need in order to worship God—can be stifling if it is not recognized and dealt with. We have, first of all, to be released from the need for special buildings consecrated for worship—and all that seems to go with them, such as a particular layout of the seating and a particular kind of seating (whether pews or hard chairs). We have also come to expect worship to take a certain form, pattern, length of time, and sequence of events. We are accustomed to certain people doing specific things up front or in familiar ways. We accept the presence and use of certain musical instruments. We assume that worship cannot happen without music. We find extended periods of silence awkward or even threatening. We like to be involved in such services of worship, but we are not sure about anything too personal or intimate. We like to leave at the end with a sense of purpose for the following week, but with a pleasant roundness about the previous sixty minutes or so. We want friendliness and a warm welcome, but it must not go too far.

Now one inevitable factor in this bundle of expectations for the worship of God's people Sunday by Sunday is the sheer size of the congregation. If you have one hundred, five hundred, or one thousand people in a specially designed building, the dynamics of the meeting become radically different from the experience of twelve people gathered in a home. It is easy to confuse these particular dynamics, and what they produce among a group of people, with the essential content of worship.

Perhaps the best definition/description of worship is contained in Paul's exhortation to the Christians of Rome: "I appeal to you therefore, brethren, by the mercies of God, to present your bodies as a living sacrifice, holy and acceptable to God, which is your spiritual worship. Do not be conformed to this world but be transformed by the renewal of your mind, that you may prove what is the will of God, what is good and acceptable and perfect" (Romans 12:1-2). Worshiping God means presenting all we are, have, and think to God as a living sacrifice. We are moved to do so because of His infinite and incredible mercies to us. We do so in order that we might discover and do His will, which is the only thing that matters and ultimately satisfies. Such a dedicated offering of our whole being to God is both costly and painful: to be a sacrifice—and a living, continuous one at that—always was and will be costly and painful.

This is the essential nature of worship, and this is what in a home group we have the privilege of discovering. Outward patterns of worship will come and go, but they are not the real thing. As members of a home group push back the boundaries of what such worship means, many exciting developments will take place. The creative juices of each person will begin to work, and imaginative ideas will emerge. These will lead to the life of a home group becoming a worshiping life, as the group discovers fresh ways of bringing their whole being before the Lord in celebration, consecration, and gradual transformation. Whatever gifts a member has can be expressed in the life of the group far more easily than in the largeness and relative anonymity of the congregation. The home group can nurture and hone the gifts of each individual in a personal way.

In particular, the meeting of a home group seems to reproduce the situation Paul envisages and encourages in his first letter to the church at Corinth: "When you come together, each one has a hymn, a lesson, a revelation, a tongue, or an interpretation" (1 Corinthians 14:26). Each person can realistically contribute to the worshiping life of home groups in one or another of these ways. It is not possible to have such contributions, except in a very limited fashion, in local congregational worship. Paul was, of course, very much aware of the dangers of abuse in such a context, but he encouraged the Corinthians to press forward.

One specific ingredient of worship is prayer. The praying life of a home group will often be the single most instructive and inspiring experience in prayer that many Christians will have. Most disciples, like the Twelve, find prayer difficult and want to be taught how to pray (see Luke 11:1). Disciples learn best with a practical example in front of them. It was watching Jesus pray that made the Twelve want to learn how to pray. The praying life of a home group can be direct, definite, and deep. By keeping a record of specific requests, we can notice the way our prayers are answered. One individual's praying can become narrow in scope and lacking in expectancy, vibrancy, and freshness. A large congregation at prayer faces problems of vagueness, remoteness, and routine. A home group is in a position to develop a corporate life that is nourished by the prayers of the group together and by the supporting prayer of each member apart from its gatherings.

One profound asset of a home group is the opportunity to "pray through" a concern or a problem. Prayer often goes only so far and then stops when you feel you are just beginning to get somewhere. This need not be so in the life of a home group. The different aspects of a person's situation can be immersed in believing, listening prayer. The listening aspect of prayer can be particularly fostered. Here again, what happens in a congregational situation has led most Christians to assume that prayer means talking to God. Prayer is the expression of a relationship, a two-way relationship. In prayer we speak to God—but God also speaks to us. The trouble is that we are so busy talking that we forget to listen.

Whatever situation comes to the attention and concern of a home group can become the focus of its complete praying attention—not simply the individual needs/desires of its members. Here the emphasis of the church near Liverpool is instructive: "We are also a community of prayer, seeking to pray for one another, for the life of St. Mary's church, for our neighbourhood, for non-Christians with whom we are in contact, for the Lord's work throughout the world."

In a home group it can become customary to bring any such situation to the Lord in prayer, to listen to what He has to say, to reach a common mind about what He wants, and then to pass on what has been learned to the appropriate leadership elsewhere, whether in that local congregation or beyond it. In London we have several times used the home groups as a sounding board for possible ways ahead for the church as a whole. As well as central times of prayer, we have asked each home group to pray specifically for God to make His way plain to and through the home groups.

Looking Inward

By looking inward, we mean the mutual support, encouragement, and care for one another that, in the New Testament, is covered by the Greek word *koinonia*. This is the common sharing in the experience of community, a feature of the earliest church in Jerusalem when they "had all things in common" (Acts 2:44, see also 4:32). The Cape Town guidelines for "house church leaders" says this:

Sharing can take place in different dimensions:

1. Ideas, concerns, feelings
2. Decisions that need to be taken by individuals or the group
3. Burdens, some of which may require practical help and support from others in the group
4. Insights or experiences from the Lord
5. Material things

Apart from meeting at the official house church meetings, it would be good to get together at other times as well on a more informal basis when children could also be involved, e.g., barbecue or picnic lunch, a day out together, or a weekend away.

It is interesting that this particular church has moved away from emphasizing the importance of sharing as such. It prefers to speak of developing relationships. This seems a significant and constructive change. Sharing can become synonymous with dumping our emotional baggage, with little or no commitment to moving forward in our relationships. It is one thing to share openly and honestly; it is quite another to be able to receive and run with what the home group then helps to lay out in front of us as a way forward.

The New Testament, especially the letters, makes plain how central this shared life became for the disciples of Jesus. A simple way to check this is to note the times Paul, Peter, John, and James use the powerful phrase "one another" — a vivid expression of Christian community life.

The church near Liverpool encapsulates the heart of this in its section on looking inward — beginning with the new commandment Jesus gave His disciples, "Love one another" (John 13:34). The leaflet continues:

Loving one another in this way involves us in laying down our lives for one another, serving one another in love: welcoming one another, listening to one another, carrying one another's burdens, praying for one another, encouraging one another in living for the Lord, using our gifts to serve one another. . . . The full expression of this love requires both our willingness to give and our willingness to ask and receive from one another.

Love is creative and imaginative, the love of God particularly so. "In a home group each person has a special opportunity to give and receive in depth the love of our Lord." Because this is the new commandment of Jesus to His disciples, we do not have an option. It becomes a question, if we do not believe a pattern of home-group life is right or realistic in our local church, whether we are sure we are obeying this new commandment in our existing life.

"As part of loving one another in this way, we seek to help one another to understand, to be encouraged by and to apply to our individual lives and in our life together the teaching of the Bible." Small-group Bible study is, of course, a common practice in many countries and in particular all over the United States. Many of the materials are most suitable for home/house churches, and it is certainly important to provide groups with skills in leading such study. Many Bible study groups share a common life in the way we have outlined in this chapter. Perhaps the major difference is in the way the home groups/house churches express and nourish the life of a local congregation. This is particularly pertinent when we come to learning and understanding the Word of God, so that we grow in our discipleship together and as individuals.

It is important to link the home group's Bible study with the exposition of God's Word Sunday by Sunday. The contexts involve different ministries: the teacher will expound the Scriptures to the congregation; the home group will wrestle, under appropriate guidance, with its specific application to the daily lives of its members. These are *both* necessary for growth toward Christian maturity. God has given people to His church as teachers; they should be encouraged and released to teach. Direct, personal, practical, specific application of God's Word can be done only in the fellowship of a group of people committed to one another in an ongoing relationship of open trust and mutual accountability. Application without exegesis and exposition is a nightmare of overspiritualization and private interpretation. Exegesis and exposition without home group application into personal lives makes the Word of God of no effect, reducing it to the level of an interesting textbook.

In his letter to the churches of Colossae, Hierapolis, and Laodicea, Paul makes his concerns clear: "Let the word of Christ dwell in you richly, teach and admonish one another in all wisdom" (Colossians 3:16). Many local churches specifically prepare, for their home groups, study questions on the scriptures being expounded Sunday by Sunday. In this way, the whole congregation is being effectively molded by the Word of God—both by a public teaching ministry and by personal application through its home groups. This need not be an imposition on the distinctive, unique life of any one home group. Any group can—and will—decide to use the materials provided as it wishes. It can put it to one side, if the consensus in the group points to some other theme or passage.

The Cape Town church, in stressing that the teaching in a house church/home group needs to be rooted and founded in the Scriptures, has a fourfold aim:

1. To cultivate in people a love for the word of God.
2. To encourage daily reading of Scripture.

3. To help people become familiar with the Scriptures and deepen their knowledge and understanding of them.
4. To help people think scripturally and apply biblical principles to form their worldview.

Paul himself used this thorough approach to teaching
the Word of God. In his farewell speech to the leadership
of the church at Ephesus, he refers in turn to three kinds of
teaching—"I did not shrink from declaring to you anything
that was profitable, and teaching you in public and from
house to house [that is, house church to house church]. . . .
For three years I did not cease night or day to admonish
every one [literally, one by one] with tears" (Acts 20:20,31).
The word *admonish* literally means to put sense into individuals: it is the same word used of the actual one-to-one ministry of teaching and admonishing that leads to the Word of
God richly dwelling in believers (see Colossians 1:28, 3:16).

Paul concludes his remarks to the Ephesian leadership
with the following: "Now I commend you to God and to
the word of his grace, which is able to build you up and to
give you the inheritance among all those who are sanctified"
(Acts 20:32). This all-round ministry of the Word of God is
as fundamental to home-group life as it is to congregational
life and the life of the individual Christian.

Looking Outward
Perhaps the greatest and most common danger home groups
is becoming completely wrapped up in their shared life,
impervious to and ignorant about the local church, the
neighborhood, national and international affairs of both
church and state. We need to work out such outward expressions of home-group life.

The first outward expression comes by developing links
with the local congregation. We have already mentioned
ways in which the two are best kept in creative interplay.

This is done through pastoral care—training and selecting of home-group leaders. It is fostered by linking Sunday teaching with home-group Bible study. As home groups multiply, shared pastoral care of leaders brings a further dimension of wider fellowship and shared responsibility. Home groups become a crucial expression—if not the major noncentral expression—of local church vision. They can be a forum for hammering out the church's perception of God's will for future growth. They act, in the natural course of their events, as fertile soil for leadership and ministry of different kinds in the congregation, as well as in the home group. As the quality of discipleship deepens in home groups, this has a spillover effect on the life of the congregation.

Home groups can serve and facilitate the life of the congregation in other ways. The single most constructive ingredient of our congregational life in London is the part played by home groups, in rotation, in the worship services of the church. Every Sunday morning and evening, one home group is responsible (with the help of one or two regular helpers) for greeting the congregation, ushering, handing out bulletins and books, taking up the thank-offering, leading the intercessions, reading the Scriptures, preparing and serving refreshments, and tidying everything up afterward. This is a demanding job and requires dedication, initiative, availability, specific gifting in different ways, sensitivity, and good teamwork. It builds up the common life and the unity of the home groups. It also spells out the interaction between home groups and congregation in an unmistakable and public way. It provides many opportunities for practical service. It often reveals budding gifts in the home groups, which can then be nurtured for wider expression in the Body of Christ.

Home groups can also take their turn at many of the practical, menial tasks that any local church faces—cleaning the building, helping in the office, supporting the catering staff, decorating the building at festivals like

Christmas and Easter, taking publicity around the neighborhood, providing meals for invalids, shopping for those
who are housebound, etc. The list can be extended indef-
initely. Such practical service automatically trains home
groups to look beyond their own needs and desires.

If the home groups have a geographical focus in a particular neighborhood, the outward look becomes a natural
expression of the daily lives of its members. Drives to
school are shared; children meet on the streets; neighbors
share their joys and sorrows while shopping; baby-sitting
abounds; parent/teacher meetings bring further interaction; friends play sports together, have a drink together,
go out for a meal together, borrow one another's tools and
books. It becomes simple, challenging, and exciting to share
one's faith in such a situation and, in particular, to plan for
appropriate times when friends and neighbors can ask their
questions and be pointed to Jesus as Lord.

This outward emphasis is important whether or not
members of the home group live close to each other. The
realities of the automobile and commuter travel have turned
many areas into neither communities nor neighborhoods
but dormitories. It is not unusual for commuters in southern California to leave home soon after 5:00 a.m. and return
after 9:00 p.m. The weekly life of a home group in such an
area, in all three of its aspects (upward, inward, outward),
needs imaginative planning, to say the least. Gathering
on the weekend and keeping in touch by telephone during the week may be a beginning. Our opportunities for
looking outward as Christians come to us daily—with our
colleagues, our fellow commuters, our golfing or tennis partners. When members of the home group bring the whole of
their living and relating into its common life, there will be
no shortage of outward-looking material.

One specific element of looking outward in home
groups is getting to grips with matters of Christian ethical
concern in the workplace and local/national life. Different

members of the home group will come into contact with different issues, and the group provides an excellent forum for study, reflection, prayer, and sometimes specific action. Although one person's specific concern may not directly affect the others, it is important to be stretched as a group to take an interest in and to make contributions to such debate. An outside speaker after a potluck supper may provide the ideal material for believers and unbelievers alike on a topic of common concern.

It is valuable for local Christians to take an active part in local, state, and national elections to political office. The issues raised—and sometimes dealt with—in political campaigning are bound to touch on convictions held by Christians and nonChristians; engaging these issues is an excellent way of opening up a home group to those who would not normally find themselves in such an open environment. We should be ready for fireworks and sharing disagreement: but experience shows that misconceptions about Christians, Christian faith, and Christ Himself can be addressed in such a meeting—or informally in the days that follow.

One of the most rewarding but challenging aspects of home-group life can be its international and missionary involvement. We have found, in three different churches over twenty years, that the best way for a whole congregation to take its international ministry seriously is to allocate each missionary or area of mission to one home group—or to more than one if the arithmetic works out that way.

We have discovered that a home group can be personal, practical, persistent, and powerful in its links with missionaries. One person is normally designated missionary correspondent, and that person's task is to ensure that the group is constantly aware of and involved in the missionary's situation—in prayer and correspondence and in sending tapes, videos, gifts, and money. Members of a home group may be in a position to visit the missionary in the field and therefore bring back direct and immediate news. The home group collectively—as much as possible—takes responsibility for the missionary on home leave.

When the home group is taking intercessions in a church service, the group's own missionary is specifically and topically prayed for. Imaginative interaction between the home group and the missionary will spawn many new ideas. The missionaries we have supported have strongly endorsed the value of these links, which invariably are firmer than those with the congregation as a whole.

This international partnership need not, of course, be restricted to links with those who go abroad in what is traditionally known as missionary work. Nowadays, some of the most significant and strategic mission is being carried out by "tentmakers"—people whose secular work takes them far and wide, fast and frequently. Very often these people can reach countries and situations where official missionaries cannot penetrate. By the nature of things, these tentmakers tend to carry a good deal of influence, and their witness for Christ can be extremely effective.

Local churches will vary in their opportunities for this kind of international outreach, but people involved in such a traveling life invariably appreciate the regular, praying support of a home group. In addition, they bring back fascinating glimpses of life—for believers and nonbelievers—in other parts of the world.

One other way for a home group to reach out is by going together on an evangelistic visit to another church. Over the years I have seen immense fruit from such projects. It may be necessary, in the early stages of such an initiative, for two or three home groups to combine forces. There is great impact in "ordinary Christians" talking about their faith in this kind of way. The event may well be a weekend spent helping members of another congregation take the gospel into their neighborhood. Sometimes a member of staff may have to take a home group on such a visit, because the invitation was made in that way in the first place. The staff member may decide to take others along as well.

We have now looked at the life cycle of a home group and at its essential aspects or ingredients. There is one yawning gap in this chapter, which now needs to be filled — leadership. All along a certain kind of leadership has been assumed. This is, as one would expect, to be along the same lines as spelled out in chapter 2 — shared leadership, servant leadership, accessible leadership, and enabling leadership. There is a New Testament word for it, especially as it is demonstrated in a home group. The word is *helmsmanship*.

SMALL-GROUP LEADERS

The Apostle Paul uses this word in 1 Corinthians 12:28 where he lists spiritual gifts and people God has appointed for specific and concerted purposes in His church. The word in question here is normally translated "administrators." Any church needs people gifted in administration. However, although the Roman Empire of the first century was no stranger to efficient administration, it is very unlikely that the word Paul uses has the connotation we now give it with our modern understanding of administrative skills.

The Greek word *kuberneseis* means "helmsman" or more precisely "acts of helmsmanship." Paul has in mind, therefore, the person who steers a ship. The helmsman knows the times of the day and of the year, the sky, the stars, the currents, the winds. He is the one qualified to direct the ship.

"The literal meaning of the word and its attested usage make it clear what Paul has in mind," wrote one commentator.

> The reference can only be to the specific gifts which qualify a Christian to be a helmsman to his congregation, i.e. a true director of its order and of its life. . . . The importance of a helmsman increases in a time of storm. The office of directing a congregation may well

have developed especially in emergencies both within and without. The proclamation of the Word was not originally one of its tasks. The apostles and teachers saw to this.[1]

God has appointed people with such gifts in His church. Helmsmen are necessary for directing the life of a local congregation and a home group. People thus gifted know both the others on board and the waters through which they are moving. They know the signs of danger and where they are heading. Helmsmen know whom to call in and when. They are sensitive to the needs of each situation and to the abilities of each individual. They can, therefore, keep the ship on course and make the best possible use of every person.

This important ministry will operate generally in the life of a home group, but specifically when it meets together. The one at the helm will sense what contribution is needed from whom and at what time. Encouragement will be given to those who are reticent about their gifts or are generally shy. He or she will be sensitive to which way the Spirit is blowing and will do everything possible to catch the full wind of the Spirit. He or she will sense when some clear word from the Lord is needed or imminent and will make space for it to be received, weighed, and absorbed. He or she will call for some definite biblical teaching when folk seem to be floundering in a welter of private opinions.

All the time the person at the helm will be working to keep the meeting on course, not in the direction the person wants it to go, but as he or she senses the Spirit wants to take it. Helmsmen will listen carefully to the suggestions of others in the group, but will not allow their eyes to be taken off the Lord. Such helmsmanship skills take time to develop; they are, almost by definition, self-effacing and inconspicuous in actual practice.

So who actually ends up *leading* the meeting (and the general life) of the home group? The Holy Spirit, as He guides the person at the helm to make full use of the gifts and ministries of every member.

We close with some suggestions about what to do with "problem people" in the home-group meetings. In general, love them, pray for them and about the problems, and be open to the Holy Spirit's leading.

1. *The talkative* (always speaking, never allowing space for others to speak):
   * Ask, "What does someone else think?"
   * Give them the job of summarizing particular discussion so that they have to listen to others.
   * Talk to them privately about the problem.

2. *The domineering* (whose voices tend to "win" over all others; they appear to brush other people aside):
   * Challenge their viewpoint by putting forward an alternative one.
   * Ask for other suggestions.
   * Break into pairs or groups of three so that everyone has the opportunity to express a viewpoint.

3. *The silent* (who never contribute anything to group discussion):
   * Try to find out the reason for the silence. Is it shyness? Reflection? Sullenness? Do they understand?
   * Give them opportunities by asking, "Does anyone want to add anything here?" or "How about those who haven't said anything so far?"
   * Take time to "bring them out" privately at another time. Personal interest and encouragement can make all the difference.

4. *The insecure* (so unsure of themselves they would tend to say, "I don't know" to every question, just so they didn't give the "wrong" answer):

* Choose an area where you know they have a contribution to make and invite them to speak.
* When they do volunteer a response, express appreciation on behalf of the group.

5. *The negative* (who get attention by deliberately standing out against others):
   * They may secretly be very unsure of themselves and be testing whether the group really accepts them.
   * Try allowing them to express their negative feelings and responding warmly and positively toward them as people.
   * Make a point, sometimes, of asking for *positive* contributions.
   * If the situation does not improve, and particularly if they have hurt others in the group, confront them with the problem — alone, if at all possible.

6. *The prickly* (easily worked up but cannot recognize their anger):
   * Allow them to express their anger, but try to help them understand the cause of it. This may mean private conversation outside the group.
   * Identify with any valid point you think they are making, and invite the group to respond positively.

7. *The red herring fisher* (constantly sidetracking discussions so that others forget the point):
   * Say "Can we follow that one up later? What about the question we were asking?"
   * Face the fact that the discussion is "off the track" and repeat the original question.

8. *The joker* (may be joking to hide embarrassment or to relieve some other tension):
   * Join in the joke, but then bring the group back to the discussion.
   * When the humor is misplaced, ignore the comment and move the discussion on.

9. *The Devil's advocate* (consistently presenting opposition even when it appears contrived):
   * They may in fact identify with the view they are expressing, or they may be doing it on behalf of someone else. It is a relatively safe way of testing opinion. Try asking if they are simply "flying a kite" or whether they are genuinely concerned.
   * Open up the discussion for the group to respond.

✳   ✳   ✳

1. To what extent do small groups in your church experience and express community life in the Spirit?

2. How can the central resources and life of your congregation be enabled to interact more creatively with the small groups linked to the church?

3. "Looking upward, looking inward, looking outward" — how are these three elements of small-group life being expressed in your church? How can they be improved?

4. In particular, what emphasis is there in your groups on participation in local, national, and international matters of Christian concern?

5. Apply the discussion of "helmsmanship" to any small groups in your church. (See pages 105-109.)

CHAPTER FIVE

LEARNING TO WORSHIP

"Those who worship God will be encouraged." This is the *Good News Bible's* rendering of Psalm 69:32. We are largely a discouraged generation because we have forgotten—or have not yet discovered—how to worship God in the way He wants and, moreover, wants to inspire us to worship. Jesus told His disciples that place and style of worship are irrelevant; what matters is that we should worship the Father "in spirit and in truth." They were in the middle of an argument, highlighted by the woman of Samaria, about the *right* place to worship God. Jesus talked of a time, ushered in by Himself, when the kind of worshipers God wanted would begin to emerge.

By the gift of His indwelling Spirit, Jesus has brought such worshiping people into the presence of God. As C. S. Lewis put it, "In the process of being worshipped God communicates his presence to men."[1] In worship we enter, touch, and are touched by the presence of God Himself. We have been created to live like that. In the words of the Westminster Catechism, "the chief end of man is to glorify God and to enjoy him forever."

People today, as in every generation, crave the real presence of God. In the German church they hold each year a *Kirchentag*, or churches' day, when church people gather together for celebration and prayer. One young German recently told me, "I have come to five *Kirchentags* looking for

God, and I have not yet found Him." That experience is, no doubt, repeated around the world. So we have the strange, sad phenomenon of people, created to worship God and live in His presence, desperately seeking God so that they can worship Him . . . *and* at the same time God Himself is seeking those who will worship Him in spirit and in truth. Where and how does the precious meeting occur?

The answer to that question, without any theological doubt or dispute whatsoever, is this: wherever the people of God meet together and, in particular, when they meet to worship the Lord, to hear His Word, and to gather around His table in the sacrament of Holy Communion. Yet week by week, day by day, these occasions turn out to be dull, empty, lifeless, and drab. Our services of worship are not necessarily encounters with the living God. The people of God come together to worship Him as Creator, Redeemer, and Sanctifier—but they often go away discouraged instead of encouraged. How can we tackle this tragedy in the church?

It needs to be said immediately that this is no easy or straightforward task. If our worship services do not send people away encouraged, the situation will not be reversed by a few cosmetic changes. Nevertheless, there are ways in which a new spirit and a different mood can be gradually brought about. The people of God need to be helped in this dimension of discipleship as in any other: We must *learn* to worship. Learning means being taught, and one early priority is to bring biblical teaching about worship to bear on the thinking of the congregation. There is possibly no single area of Christian living more prone to succumbing to the "I know what I like" syndrome than this matter of worship.

SACRIFICE

The first point to make, therefore, is that worship involves sacrifice, "a sacrifice of praise to God, that is, the fruit of lips that acknowledge his name" (Hebrews 13:15). It is costly to offer up a sacrifice of praise. In the Old Testament, King David recognized the danger and the emptiness of not seeing worship as a sacrifice when he declared, "I will not offer burnt offerings to the LORD my God which cost me nothing" (2 Samuel 24:24). We have already seen, in an earlier chapter, that sacrifice under the New Covenant involves presenting our whole bodies in spiritual worship. And yet, Sunday by Sunday, the feeling—and often the fact—is that we, as the people of God, are withholding ourselves from such a living sacrifice of praise. We go through the routine. We take part with enthusiasm in certain parts of the service, especially if we happen to like the tune or the preacher. But for long sections we are switched off and hardly involved at all in what is happening. We are spectators rather than participants, audience rather than active players.

God-Directed
The challenge from Hebrews 13:15 is actually even more pointed than we have hitherto stressed: the exhortation is "Through [Jesus] then let us continually offer up a sacrifice of praise to God." That word *continually* is the punchline. It literally means "through everything," and it is calling for us to bring absolutely everything we are, say, think, do, own, and want to God in sacrifice. We lay down ourselves on the altar. We make an offering of our very selves to God. How can we do this? "Through Jesus." Jesus has given everything for us; through Him we present everything to God. "We love, because he first loved us" (1 John 4:19).

Our worship, in a word, must be God-directed. This means weaning and winning people away from human likes and dislikes, away from a focus on the people alongside or the people up front, away from long-entrenched expectations or nonexpectations, away from ourselves, to concentrate on the Lord. It is not coincidental or circumstantial that services which comprise ministry of both Word and sacrament best achieve this concentration on God. Either the Word expounded alone or the sacrament of the Lord's Supper administered alone fails to grip and to move in the same way as when both are held together.

Communion

There are, of course, many diverse opinions about how best and how often to hold such services of Holy Communion, or the Eucharist. We need not get bogged down in details. The word *Eucharist* is full of significance, because it literally means "the good grace of God," with an emphasis on gratitude. Gratitude for grace is the foundation of worship. The worship of Heaven is focused on "the Lamb who was slain," who is worthy to receive all praise and honor from those whom He has ransomed for God from every nation, tribe, race, and tongue (see Revelation 5:6-14).

Clearly, we need the ministry of God's Word taught week by week. We also need the visual demonstration of God's grace to sinners in the bread broken and the wine poured out. Eating bread and drinking wine were—and are—the basic daily actions of people living around the Mediterranean. Jesus invested them with special significance, when He told His disciples, "Do this, as often as you drink it, in remembrance of me" (1 Corinthians 11:25; see also verses 23-24).

The first disciples began by making every meal sacramental in this special sense. Those in the Protestant tradition have veered away from the sacrament over the years, while those in the Catholic tradition have continued to emphasize not only the sacrament of the Lord's Supper, but the sacramental nature of all material things. By properly combining Word and sacrament, we can return to the apostolic and scriptural worship bequeathed to us by the Lord Himself. In the upper room on the night before He was crucified, Jesus spent much time teaching the disciples, as well as inaugurating the sacrament of His body and blood in the bread and the wine.

The emotional, spiritual, and intellectual impact today of seeing bread broken and wine poured out with this particular significance is fundamental for the encouragement of people of God. Nothing could more effectively or so movingly express the sheer grace of God in bringing sinners to forgiveness and freedom. Gratitude for such grace is the wellspring of such worship in spirit and in truth. God wants to be worshiped, to be accorded due praise and honor, to be given His worth. As we thus worship Him, we (like the elderly John in the book of the Revelation) will hear Him speaking to us, will see Him more clearly, and will feel His personal touch on our lives (see Revelation 1:17).

PRAISE

As we begin to worship the Lord in these ways, we will find we want both to praise Him and call upon others to praise Him also. All enjoyment spontaneously overflows into praise, except in the most isolated and introverted. When I find joy in something or someone, I want to give praise and call upon others to join in the praise and in the enjoyment. One of our family jokes dates back to long car journeys with all six together in some beautiful part of South Africa, the United Kingdom, or the United States of America. We would reach the top of the pass or come out of the mist into warm sunshine to see a glorious vista laid out in front of us. Before I could get the words out of my mouth, one of the children would say, with some resignation if a meal was overdue, "Another of Daddy's lovely views!" They knew I enjoyed such experiences, was bound to express praise, and wanted them to share it. It was, and is, never the same to be in a beautiful place or to have a joyful experience when there is no one to share it.

When we gather to worship God, we have so much for which to praise Him and in which to invite one another to join. Some of the best psalms and hymns give expression to this unalloyed praise. The psalmist invokes his own soul, as well as the great congregation, to praise the Lord (see Psalm 103:19-22). He calls on every living thing, "everything that has breath," to join the praise. He calls on the hosts of Heaven, the angels and the cherubim, to do what they do best—praise God.

The writer to the Hebrews paints for us a phenomenal panorama of the worshiping life of Heaven—worship we join when, through Jesus, we come in the Spirit to the New Jerusalem:

> You have come to Mount Zion and to the city of the living God, the heavenly Jerusalem, and to innumerable angels in festal gathering, and to the assembly of the first-born who are enrolled in heaven, and to a judge who is God of all, and to the spirits of just men made perfect, and to Jesus, the mediator of a new covenant, and to the sprinkled blood that speaks more graciously than the blood of Abel. (Hebrews 12:22-24)

"Praise the Lord! For it is good to sing praises to our God; for he is gracious, and a song of praise is seemly" (Psalm 147:1). Praise is good and praise is seemly. Praise is a tonic, praise is a tribute—a tonic to us, a tribute to God. The unaffected praises to the God of creation in the Psalms are an inspiration for our praises. As C. S. Lewis so finely expressed it, the psalmist's "gusto for nature" is given full scope.[2] Unlike contemporary religious ideas all around them, Jewish poets and prophets spoke of one God who created nature: "This doctrine empties nature of divinity—but also makes nature an index, a symbol, a manifestation of the Divine. Nature is an achievement of God, a great deed, a great victory (see Psalm 136). The psalmist's gusto, or even gratitude, embraces things that are of no use to man."[3] (See Psalm 104.)

Martin Luther wrote of "things that take life blithely,

like birds and babies." Where is the blithe spirit in our praise? C. S. Lewis wrote, "Praise almost seems to be inner health made audible,"[4] and in the Psalms it has all the cheerful spontaneity of a natural, even a physical, desire. The psalmist finds that he physically aches with a passion to join the great congregation in shouts of praise, especially when he has been deprived of such joy for some time (see Psalm 84).

There are, of course, several other ingredients to worship. One of the most powerful is adoration, that sense of being in the awesomeness of God's immediate presence, when He feels so close we can almost touch Him. At such times the only appropriate response is silence, even to fall prostrate in His presence. At such times words are neither appropriate nor necessary; indeed, they break into the real presence of God. It is particularly important for those responsible for services of worship to recognize and respect these holy times impregnated with the holy love of God. Instead of being nervous about them and wondering what might happen were we to break the silence, we need to be still before God and let God be God—"The LORD is in his holy temple; let all the earth keep silence before him" (Habakkuk 2:20).

It may well be that true awareness and confession of sin—another essential ingredient of spiritual worship—is kindled only by some such experience of the holiness of God. There is, of course, a place for the straightforward confession of sin in response to plain statements from Scripture about the fact and the weight of our sinfulness. One senses, however, that confession from the heart, which feels and grieves over what sin does to God, is elicited by more than an intellectual and volitional response to biblical truths. Perhaps it is only in Western, more cerebral cultures that we find it possible, indeed proper, not to be emotionally and profoundly moved in the presence of God—whether in repentance or in praise, adoration, supplication, or grief.

In other cultures today—and in the Hebrew culture reflected in the Psalms—people have what C. S. Lewis called an "appetite for God."[5] Jesus led all His disciples to believe that this appetite, this thirst for the living God, would be satisfied: "He who comes to me shall not hunger, and he who believes in me shall never thirst" (John 6:35). And yet the paradox is that the more we come to Him and the more we believe in Him, the more hungry and thirsty we become for the bread of life, the fountain of living waters. I am sure people today can have this achingly satisfying experience among the worshiping people of God.

We have not yet looked at styles, fashions, tastes; tunes, instruments, choirs; form and informality; robes, vestments, and clothing; pastors, priests and prophets, elders and deacons. This has been quite deliberate. Once we major on the fundamental essence of worship, these minor issues just listed tend to find their proper place in the overall scheme of things. This is not to say that there will not be frequent squabbles and bickering about any or all of them—but they will be obviously just that, squabbles and bickering, not fundamental issues of Christian discipleship.

PREPARATION FOR WORSHIP

It may be helpful now to look at some practical ways of encouraging the kind of worship described in the Scriptures. Much of the following deals with what can be done in preparation for worship. This is not surprising in view of the rush with which so many people invest modern life, a rush they transfer into services of worship—people hurtle into such times unprepared and unexpectant and leave surprised or even resentful that "there was nothing in that for me." We have often succeeded in dragging our times of worship down to the level and pace of our daily lives, instead of working to allow the worship to lift our daily lives into the presence and power of God. We cannot simply race into worship as we might move from one appointment to the next. There has to be preparation.

Music

Specific people need to do particular preparation. For example, the person responsible for putting the service together, whether the pastor or the music director or both together, will be aware of the immense amount of hard work involved in ensuring that, week by week, this truly is an expression of the community life of the people of God. Care will be taken to keep a balance between hymns of praise, hymns of adoration, and hymns of reflection or commitment. It is well worth taking time to go through the hymn book, making notes on the hymns that speak about God and the hymns that directly address God; the hymns that are focused on my response to God and the hymns that meditate on what God has done for me; the hymns that combine all or some of these motifs.

For example, objective hymns of praise about God include old favorites like "Praise, My Soul, the King of Heaven." This hymn, based on Psalm 103, starts with a call to oneself to praise God, declares all God has done, and ends with a summons to "angels in the heights . . . , sun and moon . . . , dwellers all in time and space." This hymn, like many others, recounts the deeds of the Lord to fellow worshipers, but does not get around to addressing God directly or personally. Hymns like "Immortal, Invisible, God Only Wise" is, strictly, a hymn of worship rather than praise, because it is addressed to God. Not all direct address is intimate; it can be awed reverence, as in that hymn.

One major discovery I made when I examined our hymn book in this way is that the oldest hymns, often translated from the Latin, include a high proportion of loving, intimate words addressed to the Lord, as in, for example, "Jesu, Thou Joy of Loving Hearts." When the Spirit has blown through the Church in renewal or revival, there seems to have been a rediscovery of this personal intimacy in worship. Both the evangelical revival in the eighteenth century and the Tractarian revival in the nineteenth century produced such hymns—for example, many of Charles Wesley's hymns, such as "Love Divine, All Loves Excelling"; or John Newton's "How Sweet the Name of Jesus Sounds"; and Frederick Faber's "My God, How Wonderful Thou Art."

The same emphasis has emerged in the songs associated with charismatic renewal in the last twenty-five years. Some examples: "You Laid Aside Your Majesty"; "As the Deer Pants for the Water"; "Father, We Love You"; and "Worthy, O Worthy Are You Lord." Some such songs actually move from statements of praise about God to direct address to Him, as in "All Heaven Declares the Beauty of the Risen Lord."

It is important for those responsible for services to know and to extend their musical repertoire. Music is not the essence of worship, but it plays a vital part in releasing God's people into praise, prayer, and penitence. The musical content of any service needs to be carefully and imaginatively balanced with the readings, the preaching, and the prayers. Most services actually have their theme already given in the subject matter of the sermon. In these cases the whole service should be planned accordingly, so that the people of God can taste something of the wholeness of worship around the theme of that Sunday. So many services are disjointed and piecemeal, with no noticeable attention given to the movement of the service as a whole.

It is certainly encouraging for a preacher to reach the place for a sermon, knowing that what has happened thus far—and what will happen afterwards—has all been properly planned to give the Word of God maximum effect. Many sermons seem to have their own life: they exist without any link to the rest of the service. This cannot but give the impression, often accurately, that the rest of the service

is not really much more than a warmup to the "real" purpose of being there—to hear the Word of God expounded.
It can, of course, give precisely the opposite message—that
is, whatever the preacher may say, those responsible for the
rest of the service have had other ideas.

If all this sounds elaborately overorchestrated, let me
hasten to add that the more time and attention given to
such preparation, the more free we are in fact to be flexible
when the time comes. The person who always stresses spontaneity and a certain kind of following the Spirit actually gets
trapped in a form and ritual of his or her own. One person, or
group of people, has very limited powers of creative spontaneity. Jesus compared scribes who had been trained for the
Kingdom of Heaven to "a householder who brings out of
his treasure what is new and what is old" (Matthew 13:52).
Something already prepared can be dropped, postponed, or
used as appropriate. Something unprepared may indeed be
inspired by the Spirit at the time. However, I am intrigued,
in working alongside people who prefer to operate with little
or no preparation, to notice how repetitive they actually
become over longer periods of time.

Personal Preparation
Some services of worship will inevitably be more structured
and predictable than others. The more unstructured it is,
the more the emphasis must fall on preparation *of* those
leading, as opposed to *by* those leading. All involved in
this vital activity need to spend good time making sure
they are right with the Lord for such leadership. Often
today the musical leadership is in the hands of a worship
group with different instruments and voices. These require
reasonably sophisticated equipment if the sound is to be
audible, let alone acceptable to a generation with highly
developed musical tastes and expertise. Long gone are the
days when a couple of microphones and an amplifier were
adequate—indeed *avant-garde*. Today, most teenagers have

modern audiovisual equipment at home (and around their heads): they soon switch off in a church that is not efficient and sensible in its use of modern technology.

All other leaders need to be equally committed to personal preparation, not just of their material and of their equipment, but of themselves and their walk with God. This is true for members of a worship group (who need, therefore, to spend time together in prayer and ministry to one another), for those leading the prayers or the notices or the service as a whole, as well as for the preacher.

In fact, everyone in the congregation could do well to prepare himself or herself more fully for worship. It is appalling how we all leave it to the last minute before getting to church. People dash in during the opening hymn, and indeed any time during the first twenty minutes or so. In some countries and cultures people are coming and going all the time, but the services of worship in these countries are more accurately measured in hours rather than minutes. There is, in fact, in such countries, a far greater sense of the family of God in the local community coming to worship the Lord on the Lord's day.

I well remember an uncanny experience one February in southern Spain. We had been kept indoors throughout the Sunday by torrential rain. By late afternoon the sun came out to herald a perfect evening. We decided to visit the old town in Marbella. The place was totally deserted. We parked at the bottom of a maze of old streets going up and across a steep hill, and we began to walk slowly up to the top. As we drew near to the top we heard singing—obviously singing in, or at least coming from, a church. We followed the singing and eventually arrived at the large parish church of Marbella. The service was being broadcast through loudspeakers on the outside of the building. We went inside the church and saw about fifteen hundred people at worship, and it seemed that the whole population of old Marbella was there. Within ten minutes the service ended and the huge congregation spilled out onto the narrow, winding streets—into homes, bars, restaurants, and clubs.

Likewise, in African countries, whole communities make their way to take part in services of worship, often traveling miles on foot to be present at, and to be part of, a time of celebration. They stay both for the worship, which often lasts four or five hours, and for the fellowship meal that invariably follows. Such an occasion will take up the whole of Sunday and no one, young or old, wants to miss out on it. One cannot help thinking that this approach to worship, which entails immense sacrifice and lengthy preparation, has much to teach us in our rushed way of life in the West.

To worship God is to taste eternity, to dwell in the presence of the One who inhabits eternity (see Isaiah 57:15). This high and lofty One, whose name is Holy, has also placed eternity in man's heart (Ecclesiastes 3:11). Created to worship God, we need to forget time in order to allow God Himself to speak and to satisfy the eternity in our hearts. We need to take time to rid ourselves of the shackles and the chains with which time has constrained us.

In practical terms, we find it invaluable to give twenty or thirty minutes to prayer before any service of worship. All involved in any way in leading the service take part in this time of prayer. It is deliberately planned to be the last thing anyone does before the service actually begins. In this way we begin to bite into the tendency to find last-minute things to do just before a service of worship. Anyone in the congregation is welcome—and warmly invited—to join in this time of prayer. We find that this acclimates us for worshiping the Lord. We pray for every aspect of the service, and we also listen to God for any specific impression or indication He may give us about what He wants to do and say during the service.

As a preacher, I can testify to the remarkable way God has confirmed very specific points of detail or application during this time of prayer. He has also, either by the same token or in another distinct way, indicated the kind of personal ministry to individuals He intends to bring, and this gives invaluable guidance and encouragement to those due to pray with any moved later to come forward to receive ministry.

EXPECTANCY

Reading this chapter, one could get the impression that I am suggesting, or at least assuming, a high degree of competence, if not skill, in leading worship. God deserves nothing but the best. If we are blessed with highly competent, indeed professional, musicians (to take one example), then we need to make sure that they bring the very best they can to the worship of God.

We are not, however, making an indirect case for nothing but the best by *human* yardsticks. In the eyes of God, the best is the best of which we, by His grace, are capable. That may well be—in fact, in the natural course of things, *will* be—something that makes people wince. Again C. S. Lewis comes to our aid. Talking about the praise of God's people, he insists that it does not cease to be true praise when, "through lack of skill, the forms of its expression are very uncouth or even ridiculous."[6]

That is why perfect praise, as far as Jesus was concerned, came from children. On the first Palm Sunday, when Jesus entered Jerusalem on a donkey,

> The blind and the lame came to him in the temple, and he healed them. But when the chief priests and the scribes saw the wonderful things that he did, and the children crying out in the temple, "Hosanna to the Son of David!" they were indignant; and they said to him, "Do you hear what these are saying?" And Jesus said to them, "Yes; have you never read,

'Out of the mouths of babes and sucklings
thou hast brought perfect praise'?"
(Matthew 21:14-16, quoting Psalm 8:2)

The psalm that Jesus quoted to those guardians of order and tradition in the temple services eloquently describes the way the whole earth declares the praise and majesty of its Creator. The heavens are "the work of thy fingers"; the moon and stars "thou hast established." All these declare the glory of God. Yet to human beings God has given sovereignty in stewardship over all the created order, so that we too can join in the continuous festival of praise going up to God day by day. Such worship, based on the glories and the intricacies of the created universe, has significant impact on the cosmic conflict between God and the forces of evil, "the enemy and the avenger" (Psalm 8:2). *Perfect* praise stills and silences the Enemy and the Avenger, even or especially when he speaks through religious bigots. On Palm Sunday it was the children who thus nullified the impact of the enemies of Jesus.

So it is clear that, when God looks for the best we can bring for *perfect* praise, He is satisfied completely with those who have no acquired skills or professional competence — so long as they give themselves, their souls and bodies, to be a living sacrifice. Children seem uniquely able thus to respond to the Lord in wholehearted praise. It does not seem to matter if they thump their tambourines out of rhythm or start the song at the wrong time. They have so much to teach us about sheer enjoyment of worship, of happiness in God.

If one word can summarize our fundamental need as God's worshiping people, it is *expectancy*. Like many churches in large cities, we face the challenge of a congregation that has many options in deciding what to do on weekends, especially on Sundays. Some have a place in the country where they prefer to go on Friday evenings, leaving the noise and grime of the city until late Sunday night, or even Monday morning. In a capital such as London, those who choose to stay over the weekend — or have no such options — have many alternative pursuits, people and places instead of worshiping with the Lord's people around the Lord's table on the Lord's day.

When we initially moved to London, we began to think of other or additional ways and times for drawing people together as the worshiping people of God. We might still possibly experiment with the option of a regular midweek expression — in corporate worship — of our life together. But, in effect, we stopped fretting about the difficulties when we realized that, if it became known that our times of worship together were filled with the presence of God and should not be missed at any price, people would make the services of worship a top priority. Now that is not true today for all the people all the time — but it certainly is increasingly true for many people most of the time. There is an air of expectancy; God is present — I am going to meet Him.

Such expectancy can neither be engineered nor — once it is around — guaranteed. It is, however, to be earnestly coveted by fervent prayer. It can be talked about, taught about. Some of the ways mentioned in this chapter can, directly and indirectly, create a climate of expectancy. The expectancy must be focused on the Lord Himself, not on any ingredient or individual. At times this focus needs to be reoriented by those in leadership.

When this expectancy is in place, there is manifest change in the lives of individual worshipers — and in the community life of God's people. As we noted at the beginning of this chapter, "Those who worship God shall be encouraged." In the different churches I have served, this has happened and continues to happen. It has been said of the Eucharistic community at worship that it is, first, a *magnet* that draws the whole community together for spiritual strength; then it becomes a *dynamo* that energizes the people of God and spins them out in service and mission. May that be true of more and more local churches.

*   *   *

1. What aspects of the worship in your church indicate or hinder a true experience of the presence of God in your midst?

2. Have you personally grown in your appreciation of worship together with the people of God in the last three years? If so, how? Why do you suppose you have or haven't?

3. What specific steps can be taken in your church to give more priority and imagination to its worship services?

4. How can we encourage one another to prepare ourselves more thoroughly to worship God?

5. If God looks for the very best we can bring to our worship, how can we avoid becoming either too concerned for professional standards or too subjective about our personal tastes?

6. Expectancy seems to be the key to growth in depth and power of worship: How can you and your church cultivate expectancy?

CHAPTER SIX

GROWING IN PRAYER

I n 1986 our church in London produced a document, which is shared with all members and newcomers, entitled "Statement of Priorities." The sixth priority is "Expectant Prayer" and reads as follows:

> We appreciate more and more the need to be in a constant attitude of prayer. We have begun to realise our own weakness and the Lord's strength. We have many anxieties and fears. We live in a frightened, violent and precarious world. As we learn to pray we expect a marked impact on situations which, in human terms, are impossible. We also recognize that prayer and planning need to be kept in continual interplay.

Years later we are still learning how to pray. We feel like newborn babies in the skill and the sweat of prayer. Like most pastors and ministers entrusted with oversight of a church, I know we do not pray as we ought or as we could. Many people in the congregation do not hesitate to say so—some to me directly and some not. We have stepped up our prayer life—by regular half nights of prayer, a weekly group for intercession, disciplined interweaving of prayer and discussion in business meetings, special calls to pray at critical times of decision making, an annual quiet day for the congregation, and other similar action.

What has become plain—if I did not in my heart of hearts know it already—is that nobody can push, bully, badger, or cajole people to pray. We either pray because we choose and actually want to pray, or we do not pray. No amount of pleading or threatening from the front or the top will move people to pray. We may get a larger turnout for two or three special occasions, normally because our future or our pockets are on the line. Then it all dies down and we realize again that we are too busy to pray.

It does not help to read books about churches that really do pray, like the amazing phenomenon in Seoul, South Korea. A church of about a million people has grown over a period of fifteen or twenty years. When you ask the pastor, Paul Yonggi Cho, for his secret, he says it is prayer. His people are up for prayer in large numbers at 4:30 a.m. every day. They even have a special prayer mountain outside Seoul, to which members go to pray for longer periods of time. I remember hearing Yonggi Cho at an international conference in the Philippines in 1989. The impact he made on us all was immense, and he stressed the central lesson of the church at prayer. But it all seemed so remote a possibility back in the reality of London. Maybe, I thought, London Christians are less disciplined than those in Seoul, and yet . . .

I realize that we can spend our time beating ourselves over the head about our weakness in prayer, ending up with such a massive guilt complex that we feel it is hardly worth praying at all. Being reasonably upbeat, I then encourage myself with familiar truths that presumably remain valid in spite of our weaknesses. The primary truth is that, because we do not know how to pray as we ought, the Holy Spirit Himself comes to the aid of our weakness and prays along with us and through us (Romans 8:26-27). As with so much, if not all, of the work of the Spirit, this presumably does not happen with any frequency unless we actually call on His help in our prayer.

The context in which the Apostle Paul explains this intercessory partnership with the Holy Spirit is even more relevant to our dilemma. Paul had been outlining the way the whole created order groans in travail, waiting in anticipation for the children of God to come into their own as coregents with the Creator of His renewed and redeemed world. We groan as well, because we know how desperately this tired old world needs the children of God to become what we are becoming. It is into this groaning that God the Holy Spirit enters in our praying. His groaning goes beyond human words, but the intercession in which He thus groans is specifically on our behalf, and it has the priceless advantage of being in line with the will of God.

It may well be, therefore, that the weakness and the groaning in our prayer life is an authentic mark of being in tune both with the creation and with the Creator. The danger comes when we opt out of this groaning, this empathy with the fallenness and the frustration of the world, and pretend to live as though it was either nonexistent, nonsignificant, or nonnegotiable. Then we really do stop praying. It is Christian hope, as Paul points out in Romans 8, that makes being human so frustrating, so fascinating, and so ultimately fulfilling.

So the bottom line in addressing the poverty of our prayer life as a church is asking the Holy Spirit to help us. In other words, in prayer we ask for help in prayer. Those of us who do pray with faith, fire, and fervor need to pray that others will want to do the same. The written accounts of revival in previous generations always highlighted the way the ground was prepared by a faithful few who kept praying when everything was bleak and hopeless.

At the very least we should, therefore, seek out the persistent intercessors in the congregation. They may not need our affirmation (or perhaps, on second thought, they do), but we should give it to them—and keep them, if anyone, in detailed touch with primary targets for prayer in the church.

We have certainly learned over the years of the immense power released, in individual lives and in the life of the church, by the confidential and private prayers of those called by God to be intercessors. Mountains have moved.

Once we have identified the intercessors, it would be wise to distribute them strategically around the home groups—although it is remarkable how the elderly, hard of hearing, and housebound, who are unlikely to be able actually to be present for a home group's meetings, tend to specialize in this crucial ministry. Perhaps it would be strategic to apportion one home group to intercessory support by one such elderly Christian.

ACTIVISTS AT PRAYER

If, in prayer, we are practicing the presence of God, it is especially important that the more active and energetic among us learn how to pray. Nehemiah is the best example of such a person. He was an intensely practical man—he got things done. When confronted with a mammoth task—such as rebuilding the city wall at Jerusalem after it had lain in ruins for seventy years—he organized his labor force so effectively that the work was completed in fifty-two days (Nehemiah 6:15). But Nehemiah was also a man of prayer. This is mentioned or described thirteen times in the thirteen chapters of the book.

The whole project was conceived in prayer, commenced in prayer, continued in prayer, and completed in prayer. For example, at the outset we read: "When I heard these words [that the wall of Jerusalem was broken down and its gates destroyed by fire] I sat down and wept, and mourned for days; and I continued fasting and praying before the God of heaven" (Nehemiah 1:4). When he went to King Artaxerxes at the start of his project, in order to get the necessary permission and provisions, the king said to him: "For what do you make your request?" Nehemiah's own account then reads, "So I prayed to the God of heaven" (2:4). Once in Jerusalem and with the wall well under way, the next major obstacle was continued opposition from the Samaritans in the land: "What are these feeble Jews doing?" Nehemiah at once turns the taunts over to God in prayer: "Hear, O our God, for we are despised; turn back their taunt upon their own heads" (4:4). The end of the task and of the matter for Nehemiah is similarly focused in prayer: "Remember me, O my God, for good" (13:31).

Nehemiah prayed as he worked. He prayed before, during, and after crucial decisions, important interviews, difficult situations. He wept in prayer; he rejoiced in prayer. He spent long periods in prayer and he shot off arrow-prayers when there was no time for anything else. He prayed both under attack and when achieving his goals.

Nehemiah had a heart to pray. What did this bring him? First, he came to know God better. Three phrases used in the book of Nehemiah provide us with clear insight into the personal relationship he had with the Lord. Three times he talks about "the God of heaven" (1:5; 2:4,20). Nehemiah's God was above all the hassles and hatred of people on earth; this God saw it all and governed it all in accordance with His eternal counsel. His God was no national, or even imperial, divinity; He rules over kings, governors, generals, and even civil servants. This God's resources, as well as His responsibilities, were directed from the throne of Heaven to meet the situations on earth as He thought fit. Nehemiah knew God to be this God, because he spent time consulting Him and listening to Him in prayer.

The second and third phrases Nehemiah uses of the Lord go together and are equally eloquent: "my God" (2:12, 6:14), "our God" (4:20, 5:9). When concerned for his own safety and integrity, he refers to "my God"; when concerned to help his people keep faith and act justly, he speaks to them of "our God." He was equally in touch with the Lord in his personal life and as a spokesman for the Lord in front of the people of God. In prayer he had come to know the Lord in both dimensions—he did not let his personal relationship ride on the back of his leadership of God's people. Nor did he allow his awesome calling to leadership absorb completely his relationship with the Lord. This balance is extremely hard to keep up in Christian work.

KNOWING WHAT GOD WANTS

As he came to know "the God of heaven" as "my God" and "our God," at least three things became real for Nehemiah. First, *he knew what God wanted*: God wanted the Jerusalem wall rebuilt. This was by no means a foregone conclusion—God might have wanted the wall, the Temple, and the city to remain devastated for several years or generations or even forever. He might have wanted a completely new city built on a new site altogether. Nehemiah knew the prophecies, but as centuries of Hebrew, Arab, and Christian exegesis have painfully shown, they are anything but precise: you can draw most conclusions at will if your heart is set on something or your mind already made up.

Nehemiah reached this conviction that God wanted the wall rebuilt as he prayed and opened himself up to God's own heart. In chapter 1 this absorption with the Lord's feelings about Jerusalem is fully and movingly described. Nehemiah identifies completely with the sins of his forefathers—he confesses the sins of his people now. He confesses the sins of his family and those of his own life. He acknowledges that God is a great and terrible God, and yet a God who keeps covenant and steadfast love with those who love Him and keep His commandments. He then recalls the basis of that covenant, expressed to and through Moses, and pleads for practical mercy now and on behalf of those whom God has so signally and mightily redeemed from forces that had overwhelmed them. "O Lord, . . . give success to thy servant today" (1:11).

It is equally important that those entrusted with responsibility for the work and the people of God spend time in prayer attuning themselves, and where necessary, adjusting to what God wants. We cannot assume that we know this. Certainly we have general instructions from Jesus, the Head of the Church, that tell us to go and make disciples of all the nations, baptizing them and teaching them all that He Himself has commanded (Matthew 28:18-20). We also have His own declaration of intent: "I will build my church" (Matthew 16:18), coupled with His own promised presence, "I am with you always" (Matthew 28:20), and the gift of the Holy Spirit (Luke 24:49). But how, when, where? Are the answers to these questions so self-evident that we can afford to plow on before spending time in prayer with the God of Heaven? Jesus expressly stated, in giving His disciples the Great Commission before He ascended into Heaven, that "all authority in heaven and on earth has been given to me."

If Jesus possesses that kind of authority, if He is God of Heaven and earth, if He is our God and my God, then He alone knows how best to build His church in central London; in Cape Town; in the Midwest or the Deep South; in New England or California; in urban ghettos or rural communities; among business executives or migrant laborers.

The pressure on any church leader, especially upon coming new into a situation (but it never recedes), is to bring in a plan of campaign as soon as possible, a vision of what is wanted, goals to aim for and priorities for action. It is intriguing that Nehemiah would not say anything to anyone about what God wanted until he had completed a thorough reconnaissance of the situation (Nehemiah 2:11-16). Indeed, taking only a few intimate colleagues, he carried out this inspection at night, so that no one knew what he was doing. Nehemiah clearly wanted to be sure of the facts as well as the will of God.

This combination of knowing God and knowing the situation is highly impressive. In recent years I have found myself going wrong on both counts. I can think of plans to recover and renovate an old building, once used by the church but subsequently rented out because it was no longer needed. I believe I heard God correctly about the need to bring the building back into church use: I consulted Him about it and came to know what He wanted. But I did not do my homework on the condition of the building, our contractual obligations, the cost of proposed alterations, and the availability of financial resources.

Equally, I can think of more than one situation where we have thoroughly investigated the facts of the matter, but have not spent enough time consulting the Lord in prayer about what He wanted. It all seemed so obvious that prayer was superfluous, almost an expression of doubt rather than trust. Very often such situations are all about timing: does God want this now or later? That was part of Nehemiah's problem. I now have a warning signal that goes off in my spirit quite frequently — "The right idea but the wrong time." Only prayer will sensitize us to what God wants and when He wants it.

KNOWING WHAT GOD WANTS FROM US

The second result of Nehemiah coming to know God better in prayer is that he knew what God wanted *from him*. There is an eloquent little phrase later in the story. The work was proceeding apace; the opposition had been repelled, but they were not going to let Nehemiah carry on unimpeded. So they switched tactics — from direct assaults to subtle invitations. "Come and let us meet together in one of the villages in the plain of Ono," they said. Nehemiah's reply is both instructive and intriguing: "I am doing a great work and I cannot come down" (6:3).

Nehemiah knew God wanted him to concentrate on the work of rebuilding the wall, and by this stage the wall had been built to the point where there was no breach in it; all that was needed was to set up the doors in the gates. The bulk of the work was over and only the finishing touches remained. Nehemiah himself was hardly needed to supervise these last few matters, and he could afford to take time to improve public relations. These characters had made life very difficult, but they did live in the neighborhood and the people of God would have to live with them. It would have made good sense to win them over and come to some kind of reconciliation.

But Nehemiah knew, because he was a man of prayer, what God wanted *from him*. He was not to be diverted. If talks with these men were appropriate, then someone else would have to do it. He was prepared to tackle only what fitted in with what God wanted him to do. He was ruthless in cutting out activities and responsibilities that took him away from his primary task.

It is probably true that more of God's work is hindered or aborted because Christian leaders fail to say no to competing interests than for any other single reason. Nehemiah was adamant: "I am doing a great work and I cannot come down." If God has given us our work, then it is a great work and we must *not* allow ourselves to be sidetracked. For me personally, my present work is to teach the Word of God and to enable the leadership of the church. I am gradually, amid the pain of unlearning habits ingrained over the years, divesting myself of other responsibilities and delegating those (hopefully *not* dumping them) elsewhere. Others are finding the call of God to do that work. So, for them, it becomes "a great work," when to me it is a burden and a diversion.

KNOWING WHAT GOD WANTS NEXT

The third result of Nehemiah's life of prayer was that he knew what God wanted *next*. In 2:12 we read that Nehemiah at the outset had discerned "what my God had put into my heart to do for Jerusalem." In 7:5 he remarks, "Then God put it into my mind to assemble the nobles and the officials and the people to be enrolled by genealogy." So in prayer Nehemiah discovered the overall plan of God *and* he discovered the next step in the process.

All kinds of thoughts pop up into our minds—how can we tell whether they are from God or not? Nehemiah developed a sensitivity through walking and talking with God. As he dug deep into the presence of God, he came to recognize the voice of God—just as sheep learn the voice of their shepherd.

I am writing this in a beautiful, tranquil valley in the Pyrenees in southwest France. When the time comes for the sheep to go home for the night, the shepherd calls the "lead sheep" by name from as far as three hundred yards away. Immediately the sheep hurries to him, followed at once by the whole flock. Nobody else can call that sheep by name; it responds to no other voice except that of its shepherd. Nehemiah came to know, almost instinctively, when God was speaking to him, or whether it was either his own idea or the voice of an enemy.

This facility is fundamental, and there is no fail-safe way of guaranteeing it. It is the fruit of a living, growing relationship with the God of Heaven, who has come to be my God and whom, along with and on behalf of the people of God, we discover to be our God.

It is good to realize that, in knowing what God wanted next, Nehemiah knew all he needed to know. We spend a lot of time fretting and dreaming about what will happen a long way down the track, especially if we are of a visionary and strategic inclination. We lie awake at night trying to work things out in detail, hatching plans for the coming months and years. It is good to have plans; it is necessary that all our plans are provisional; it is important to know what is the next step. Once we have taken this step, God will make it plain what the next one is.

Before we move on to consider another major result of Nehemiah's life of prayer, let us pause to take in the sheer size of the task God put into Nehemiah's heart and responsibility. It was no minor challenge to travel from Susa, capital of the mighty Persian empire, over a thousand miles back to a devastated city, from which he may have been deported as a young man (if he had been alive at the time) many years previously. He had to take on the rebuilding of the city wall with a group of his fellow countrymen. He had to get permission, not only from the king of Persia, but from provincial governors and lesser civil servants in the imperial bureaucracy. He had to find, gather, and arrange the transportation of huge amounts of raw materials. He had to sustain everyone's morale when the work became less than straightforward because of enemy action. He had to deal with internal bickering and shady dealings among his own people. And he had to ensure that everyone was fed adequately.

We may well find that today we are facing a task that seems equally immense—if not impossible. Only a life of prayer on par with Nehemiah's will keep us steadily moving ahead. We too will have to deal with logistical, organizational, inspirational, emotional, and ethical challenges such as Nehemiah faced—although probably on a smaller, more local scale. He knew that God wanted the community life of His people restored. God wants the same today in every city, neighborhood, and village.

It is still remarkable how God moves secular authorities to make decisions that, contrary to all human precedent and logic, make possible the work of the Spirit. Sometimes this happens as doors are opened for planning permission or the like. Sometimes God moves to block ideas we have, and we are forced by bureaucratic delays or opposition to rethink or repray through that situation. We later find that, however frustrating the attitude of officialdom at the time, God was behind their intransigence or their inefficiency.

We should not, therefore, be afraid to "think big," so long as we are keeping close to the Lord in prayer and are genuinely prepared to have our personal desires and ambitions consigned to the scrap heap. We can be sure of one thing: God's plans for His church in our neighborhood are bigger and better than ours.

KNOWING PEOPLE

Nehemiah came, through prayer, to know God better. He also came to know *people* better, and he came to know himself better. He came to know his friends better and who his true friends were. He came to know his foes better, and he came to know those who pretended to be friendly but were actually opposed to him. This was the case with one Shemaiah, the son of Delaiah (6:10). As Nehemiah absorbed the advice Shemaiah gave him, he sensed that the man was not all that he appeared to be. Nehemiah concludes: "I understood and saw that God had not sent him" (6:12).

In any work of God, sound judgment of people is essential. Every work of God means teamwork. Teamwork is, as we have seen in the ministry of Jesus, a painful and problematic way to walk. On many occasions it must have crossed the Lord's mind that He would be better off on His own. It was only after a night of prayer that He chose the Twelve (Luke 6:12-16). He saw them as the men His Father had given Him (John 17:6,9,24).

Nehemiah, in and through prayer, was careful about the people he consulted, conscripted, and coordinated. The story is full of his insights into the way people tick and the way they react in particular circumstances. In the long list of workers assigned to particular tasks in chapter 3, we come across this shrewd comment: "Next to them the Tekoites repaired; but their nobles did not put their necks to the work of their Lord" (3:5). Later, he makes the intriguing observation about a key worker called Shallum who "repaired, he and his daughters" (3:12) — the only women in the work force, apparently.

There is another refrain in this list that indicates Nehemiah's knowledge of people. Several individuals or groups "repaired opposite his house" (3:10,23,29-30) or "beside his own house" (3:23). Our motivation is that much greater and more durable if we are repairing our own property. Similarly, it looks as if Nehemiah put the leaders in charge of the areas of the city that they historically governed: "Hashabiah, ruler of half the district of Keilah, repaired for his district" (3:17; see also verse 18).

Unless Nehemiah had been concerned to know his leadership well, he would not have known their names or the details of their work sufficiently to record it in writing. He recognized the supreme value of personal attention to individuals with responsible positions. He would not, presumably, have been able to know everyone's job in specific ways — or even the name of each worker. But he kept close to his team of leaders.

Nehemiah was also a wise and skilled leader when dealing with the people as a whole. We have several examples of this invaluable gift. At the beginning of the operation, he withheld any public announcement about his campaign for three days. During that time the people would have wandered around the city, taking in the devastation and feeling in their souls the desolation and the disgrace in front of their eyes. In the meantime, Nehemiah carried out a more deliberate, strategic inspection during the night.

When the people had tasted the bitterness of the situation, only then did Nehemiah tell them about what God had put in his heart, how Artaxerxes had responded to his requests, and that "the hand of my God . . . had been upon me for good" (2:18). The response was immediate and intense: "Let us rise up and build." By his shrewd understanding of his people, Nehemiah was able to unite them all — "the priests, the nobles, the officials, and the rest that were to do the work" (2:16). Nehemiah's comment at this stage is self-effacing, but speaks volumes about his people skills: "So they strengthened their hands for the good work." He could properly stand before his critics and his enemies and properly use the first-person plural, not the "royal we" — "The God of heaven will make us prosper, and we his servants will arise and build" (2:20).

It takes a lot of prayer, and a lot of determination born of prayer, to be the kind of leader who trusts in the people as a whole to reach sound, united decisions about the "good work" of the Lord. It is not manipulation for people in leadership, like Nehemiah, to use their knowledge of and their skill with people to effect the best conditions for popular consensus. After all, it is the people who are going to "do the work." Priests (and pastors), nobles (and elders), and officials (and deacons) come and go. Any true work of God is from, by, and for the people of God.

FEAR

The one predominant factor in all personal relationships and in all people management is *fear* — fear of getting or doing it wrong; fear of losing face or position; fear of consequences; fear of discovery; fear of failure; fear of authority; and fear of what other people think, say, or do. As Christians we can add fear of missing out on God's will, fear of being rejected finally and eternally, fear of what lies beyond death, fear of discovering that it has all been an illusion anyway.

Nehemiah faced fears of all kinds, and he also discovered the only proper, healthy fear — fear of God. He mentions this once explicitly, but it was probably a developed habit in his own daily behavior. When he was appointed by King Artaxerxes to be governor in the land of Judah, he could have continued the practice of his predecessors, who had given themselves a hefty food allowance as one perk of the job. This had entailed placing "heavy burdens upon the people" in order to live in the style to which they had become accustomed.

The first thing Nehemiah did as governor was to refuse this special allowance, and then he also refrained from putting in a large expense account for the entertaining he inevitably incurred. His hospitality was lavish by any standards, but he paid for it out of his own pocket. In both these ways Nehemiah adopted a lifestyle considerably less lavish than he could have chosen—a decision to which he adhered "because the servitude was heavy upon this people" (5:18).

But a deeper reason for Nehemiah's conduct was this: "I did not do so, because of the fear of God" (5:15). Because he was constrained by this fear, he was able to bring pressure to bear on the people to behave in the same spirit. When there was a lot of self-interested, greedy profiteering among those who engaged in the restoration work, he challenged everyone involved directly: "The thing that you are doing is not good. Ought you not to walk in the fear of our God?" (5:9).

"The fear of the LORD is clean, enduring for ever," declared David (Psalm 19:9), absorbing the majesty of the God whose glory the heavens are constantly proclaiming. When David was in an extremely frightening situation, he had learned how cleansing and liberating, as well as creative and ingenious, is this fear of the Lord. He meditates on it in another psalm: "O fear the LORD, you his saints, for those who fear him have no want!" (Psalm 34:9). A paraphrase of this verse, in the hymn that begins "Through all the changing scenes of life," puts it like this: "Fear him, you saints, and you will then have nothing else to fear."

As Nehemiah learned, through his life of prayer in the presence of God, what it meant to fear the Lord, he was able to see when others tried to play on his potential fears in order to distract him from the good work of the Lord. He recognized, for example, that Sanballat and Tobiah (and several others) were all the time attempting to frighten him. Four times in the space of one chapter this is mentioned—"They all wanted to frighten us," "He was hired that I should be afraid," "The prophetess Noadiah and the rest of the prophets wanted to make me afraid," "Tobiah sent letters to make me afraid" (6:9,13-14,19).

These individuals used all the usual scare tactics of the enemy. They invented reports for public consumption, to the effect that Nehemiah was intent on building his own kingdom, not restoring God's Kingdom. This report took the form of an open letter with wide circulation, which just happened to fall into Nehemiah's hands, with the threat that Artaxerxes would be hearing about it all. Letters then and now can be a very frightening method of putting us off the work of God. In recent months I have had several such missives, all with the intention of trying to abort what God has shown He wants to bring about.

The other group of scaremongers is also very contemporary. They were either prophets or prophetesses, and they claimed to use their assumed gift of prophecy to persuade Nehemiah to step out of line. But because he kept close to the Lord, he was not swayed, let alone taken in, by their messages. As he prayed and listened to God, he realized that these folk had not been sent by God and were in no sense speaking from or for Him.

You have to be quietly confident in your own relationship with the Lord if you are going to stand firm against any who use spiritual artillery to deflect you from your God-given priorities. Over the last twenty years or so, I have felt very pressured by (usually) godly people who come on strong with "what the Lord wants for this church." Sometimes the tone is flattering ("You are the person God has chosen to . . ."); at other times the tone is condescending ("This church is dead and God has lost patience with you").

Nehemiah took such words straight to the Lord in prayer, just as he had taken the letters to the Lord. In prayer he realized who his friends were and who his actual enemies were. So, when it came to choosing someone to have overall charge of Jerusalem once the wall had been completed, he looked for a man like himself who had learned to fear God. "I gave . . . Hananiah the governor of the castle charge over Jerusalem, for he was a more faithful and God-fearing man than many" (7:2).

It might perhaps be good, therefore, for us to take a long look at the work God has given us to do in rebuilding the people of God, and to ask the Holy Spirit to highlight for us any ways in which fear, the wrong kind of fear, is influencing our decisions and behavior. Have we honestly learned the cleansing, liberating aspect of fearing God alone? If we have in the past, is it in place today? People outside and inside the church can both play on our fears. Almost like wild animals, certain people can sense when we are afraid and what makes us afraid. These people can be merciless, because they do not want to see the work of God succeed.

If, however, we hang in there in the place of prayer with the Lord, He will see to it that we do succeed in the good work He has inspired and planned. When that happens — and is generally *seen* to have happened — the boot is on the other foot. Look at what happened to Nehemiah: "So the wall was finished . . . in fifty-two days. And when all our enemies heard of it, all the nations round about us were afraid and fell greatly in their own esteem; for they perceived that this work had been accomplished with the help of our God" (6:15-16).

*   *   *

1. How would you evaluate the prayer life of your church — corporately and individually?

2. Especially noting the experiences of Nehemiah, work out what you and your church need to do to discover God's will for your life together.

3. How can prayer become practically more central to the decision-making process in your church?

4. Do you know the experience of being put off, even paralyzed, by those who seem to have a hotter line to God than you do? How do you feel about that and about them?

5. Is fear, of the wrong kind, having any influence on your life and work with the people of God? How?

CHAPTER SEVEN

MOVING TOWARD WHOLENESS

A s well as being a learning community, a worshiping community, and a praying community, the local church is also intended by its Head to be a healing community. Jesus sent His disciples out to heal, with the same mission and the same authority as Himself. It is sad that the imperative in this ministry has been muted in debates and divisions about the legitimacy, in today's world of medical sophistication in technology and in treatment, of the church expecting to see physical healing through prayers alone.

WHOLENESS IN PHYSICAL HEALING

Cautions

Those who narrow the ministry down to this issue do not always miss the point, but they often can't see the wood for the trees. Nobody would, or could, dispute several facts: one, that the medical profession in the 1990s can minister healing in a way people like Dr. Luke, for example, could never have dreamed possible. Two, many—if not most—of those who went to Jesus and the apostles for healing would today end up at the local surgery or hospital, and that is the work of God as much as was the healing ministry in the gospels and the Acts of the Apostles. Three, what the medical profession can achieve today merits the word *miraculous* as much as the acts of healing performed two thousand years ago by Jesus and the apostles.

Several other factors, rather than facts, can be readily acknowledged. One, the world of first-century Palestine was not exactly well endowed with medical resources and expertise; the same situation is prevalent in Third-World countries today. There it is, *prima facie*, likely that the God who wants to heal—as Jesus made absolutely plain—will readily bring His healing without medical means to people who have no access to them.

Two, in today's world (as in the world of Jesus and the apostles) there is a widespread and pervasive belief in magic, recourse to occultism, and acceptance of the supernatural. There will, therefore, be an inevitable interaction between the practice of the magic arts and the practice of Christian prayer—and that in a way that requires care, tact, and discernment.

Three, there always has been—and presumably always will be—a fascination with the extraordinary and the dramatic. There also has always been a desire to be healthy, not sick—except in rare cases when that condition is itself unhealthy. People will always, therefore, be drawn to any potential source of healing without any necessary willingness to move from healing toward faith in the healer. We can expect, then, superficial and sensation-seeking people to proliferate around places of healing.

It is important, furthermore, to be clear that there have been countless claims to physical healing, through Christian prayer, that have not been medically substantiated, and many that have been specifically invalidated after due lapse of time, or could have been attributed to trends observable in similar cases and are actually remissions, not healings. In addition, physical healing without recourse to medical means has never been the prerogative of the Christian church. Healing takes place in all kinds of religious or spiritual contexts: so there is nothing essentially Christian about healing as such.

The Lord's Commission

After making due allowances for all these facts, factors, and findings (and there are many more where those came from), I must make my own position clear. I believe in and accept the Lord's commission to His Church to be a healing community. I am convinced that this includes the power to heal people physically, and that this is not to be confined to the medical profession. I am equally convinced that the commission to heal is not—nor was it ever intended by Jesus to be—simply a mandate to heal people physically. Jesus was, and remains, concerned for and committed to the salvation of men, women, and children—salvation including realities (in biblical categories) such as healing, deliverance from demonic forces, forgiveness, wholeness, holiness. In commissioning the Church in His name to preach the gospel of the Kingdom, to heal, and to cast out demons, Jesus was entrusting to the Church the fullness of the Kingdom of God. If a local church fails to include healing—through direct prayer and/or in cooperation with the local medical practitioners—in its overall ministry, it is being disobedient to the Lord and is thereby shortchanging those who are hungry for God.

I make these unequivocal statements on the basis of biblical teaching, not on the basis of my personal experience—although in fact my own experience substantiates the teaching of the Bible, both in the spiritual Body of Christ in churches where I have served, and in my own physical body, in which I have known physical healing on two manifest and marvelous occasions.

Those who put to one side this scriptural teaching, including those who attempt to isolate healing and other miracles within the Apostolic Era, are actually basing their convictions on experience, not on the Scriptures. There is nothing in the New Testament to give us warrant to assert that the Lord intended miracles of healing to cease with the apostles, and to be replaced by the canon of

Scripture. Yet we still have strong assertions that this *is* what God intended . . . and that they, anyway, have never seen such miracles in their own lives. That is an argument from experience — or lack of experience to be precise. But we cannot walk all over Scripture and thrust aside the essential commission of our Lord Jesus Christ because of our lack of personal experience and our particular "reading-in" to the text what is manifestly not there. The plain sense of Scripture (one of the planks of the Protestant Reformers) must prevail.

I also want to make it clear that I am not hereby endorsing each and every, or any one particular, method of bringing healing into the life of the Church. I am concerned to be obedient to the commission of the Lord and to release the full ministry of the Church in and to the world — a ministry of healing; casting out all demons; teaching all that Jesus commanded us; baptizing in the name of the Father, Son, and Holy Spirit; and preaching (literally, *heralding*) in this way the good news of the kingly rule of God in Jesus Christ. I hope, in the rest of this chapter, to give a few clues as to how a local church can thus be a healing community.

Keep a Wide Context
First and foremost, we need to ensure that the gospel focus on salvation, full and free, is maintained throughout the life of the local church — in its services of worship, in the life of the home groups, in personal counseling, in evangelism, in training and development of leadership. This entails, negatively, not letting healing as such become either a specialist or separate issue — specialist for those who like that sort of thing, or separate from the mainstream of church life. It is helpful, in order to catch the force of our Lord's own example in this matter, to encourage a straightforward read through the gospels and the Acts of the Apostles.

From this priority will flow other emphases. For example, it is not helpful or wise to restrict a ministry of healing either to one place and time, or to one particular group of people. Home groups are excellent for helping individuals open up about personal *dis*-ease or disintegration, for which they want to ask for healing and wholeness. But it is good, also, to encourage individuals who have thus asked for prayer in the home group to come forward in a worship service for anointing with oil by leaders. Similarly, those who come for anointing in a worship service are best encouraged also to share what the Lord is doing in their lives with their home group—or at least with the leaders of the group, if at this stage the matter is too private.

It is important also to keep any question of healing firmly in the context of the Lord's purposes for the *whole* of the person's life and being. Very often, physical or emotional dis-ease is symptomatic of something deeper. Even when there is no specific or discernibly direct connection with a deeper, underlying problem, illness or weakness can become the springboard for a much fuller work of God in a person. The instructions in James 5:14-20 are fascinating in this regard. James begins by asking if "any among you" is sick. In the next six or seven verses he ranges far and wide, even harking back to Elijah as an inspiration for fervent prayer, and moving from salvation, through forgiveness, to healing. He is quite unabashed in assuming that anyone who is sick will probably need "the full works," and he ends the advice—and the whole letter—with an urgent plea to bring back any backslider. The implication is that this particular dimension might also be present in prayer for healing the sick: certainly the same emphasis on salvation and forgiveness comes in his instructions.

If we keep the ministry of healing in the wider, fuller context of the Lord's perfect will for the individual and for His people, several other perspectives emerge. We see, for example, that the church itself is part of the Lord's provision for healing—through its worship, fellowship, teaching, and prayers. It also becomes more plain that physical healing is not the be-all and end-all: people can cope far better with the absence of healing or with delayed healing, if they are being loved and ministered to in the ongoing life of the Body of Christ. Conversely, the faith and love of God's family is itself a healing force, both creating faith and love in the individual and sustaining him or her in the determination to hold on until light begins to shine in the darkness.

Cooperate with Medical People
A further consideration needs to be taken into account: the importance of developing, as far as possible, cooperation between the local church and the local medical practitioners. There is immense benefit all around if the two can establish and maintain a partnership in healing. It is of great value, of course, if local doctors, specialists, psychiatrists, psychologists, etc. are involved in the life of the church. They can initiate a working relationship, in conjunction with the leadership of the church. When we were in Cape Town, one of the most encouraging developments was the way such cooperation gradually—and it will always be gradual—built up. First, a local general practitioner decided to ask patients who were members of his church whether they would like him to inform or even consult with the pastor. Invariably they were only too happy to do so.

This lead was then taken up by another member of the church, a consultant psychiatrist. Gradually a fuller appreciation of the distinctive, but complementary, contributions from the two professions began to grow. The process began with the initiatives taken by the medical professionals, although in both cases there had been a fair degree of informal chat over coffee at the end of services or in each other's homes.

There is much misunderstanding, and at times it can only be called paranoia, about the relationship between the spiritual and the medical approaches to sickness and healing. We all know of horror stories about chronically ill people who have gone forward for healing at a "special" service, only to be told to stop all medication as an act of faith. This total dichotomy between the two approaches can make even the most open person deeply skeptical. It may, on occasion, be right for a person to come off medication; but surely this must be in full consultation with the doctor concerned.

It is worth mentioning at this point, almost in passing, that those in the medical profession are far more open to such partnership than we might sometimes be led to believe, not least those who have no Christian allegiance. I well remember a Jewish consultant in a psychiatric hospital in Cape Town who was looking after a young woman who had made several attempts at suicide. I went to the consultant's office before seeing her, both to receive permission to enter the closed ward and because I had never met her—her mother had phoned me out of the blue and asked me to visit her. The consultant was very frank and unusually detailed in our conversation, concluding with the following statement: "You know, padre, her fundamental problem is guilt, and there is nothing we can do about that . . . it's over to you." I wish to God the story had a happy ending, but tragically the woman's next suicide attempt was successful.

I do not know whether the young woman ever found peace with God. But I do remember another, younger still, who was the first person I (consciously) encountered who was suffering from anorexia nervosa. She was a most strikingly beautiful girl of about fifteen when we first met her. She came from a devastated and devastating family background, hardly ever saw her parents, was willful and rebellious, and seemed to have no time or room for God. She was the despair—and the joy—of her devoted foster mother. She was using drugs and gradually stopped eating. From being a shapely young teenager she was reduced to skin and bones.

This process took about six months, during which time she was often away for days on end, occasionally phoning her foster mother to touch base. We saw her in our home hardly ever, and never in church. Then, suddenly, she appeared at a service on her own, looking like a wraith, so utterly different that I actually did not recognize her until she told me who she was. She came back for two more Sundays, as I recall. It was then Easter Day, and she had found the Lord to be alive, alive for and in her. There was a special radiance around her fragile body. She had found salvation. By Tuesday she had died. It is one of those stories, of which there are countless in every community, for which there is no adequate rationale. We felt like the Jews in Bethany when Lazarus had died: "Could not he who opened the eyes of the blind man have kept this one from dying?" (John 11:37).

Yet, for her, death was the Lord's healing. She was prepared to die, because she had begun to taste the life of the risen Lord. We wanted her, desperately wanted her, to go on living with us and to begin to discover what it could be like here on earth. But the Lord thought otherwise, and He knows what He's doing. The local church did become for her the healing community—sacrificially, steadily, sorrowfully in the love of her foster mother, and sacramentally in the joyful celebration of Easter. If our faith in Christ cannot help us die well, what is the point of looking for healing? The reality of resurrection is the triumph of God's healing activity in the world, and our resurrection bodies will make that gloriously plain.

These stories—and there could be countless others—pinpoint the massive tension of living in God's fallen world as redeemed sinners. Any ministry of healing must honestly proceed and develop with this tension. The temptation is to go easy on the healing side and to go along with the mortality emphasis—or, for some, the temptation is to ignore and forget the "failures" and to publicize the "successes." Perhaps a better way is to ask for grace to live in the tension with integrity and proper obedience to our Lord's commission.

WHOLENESS IN SPIRITUAL HEALING

This also brings into focus the question of how much we have a right to expect from God on this side of eternity. I want to return to this in more detail in the next chapter, especially in terms of what we teach about God, His Kingdom, and His own suffering. For now, it will be worth looking more widely at the healing of relationships, of trauma and memories from the past, of deep-seated attitudes and instinctive reactions: Is the redeeming power of God to be experienced in these areas? And, if so, to what extent and in what way?

Let us start by returning to the biblical understanding of healing. It applies to people and to nations, to the land, to its waters, to broken hearts, to relationships, to diseases, to backsliding. Healing, biblically, covers our attitudes, our emotions, our mind, our imagination, our intellect, our will, our understanding, our memories, and our bodies. Healing is part of God's grace in making us whole and holy. As we have noticed, the umbrella word is *salvation*.

When we use the language of redemption, therefore, we are automatically into the meaning and the scope of the cross of Jesus. If our salvation means healing in that all-embracing sense, how does the death of Jesus bring our redemption, a word meaning "to be released from the grip of something or someone"? The biblical writers consistently declare that such a release has been achieved through the death of Jesus. Perhaps the clearest, and for our purposes, the most explicit summary comes from Simon Peter: "You know that you were ransomed from the futile ways inherited from your fathers, not with perishable things such as silver or gold, but with the precious blood of Christ, like that of a lamb without blemish or spot" (1 Peter 1:18-19).

Whether Peter was writing to Jewish Christians or Gentile Christians, or to a mixture of both, living in what we know as Turkey, need not detain us. The particular ways they had inherited from their fathers would have had a certain amount of specific reference, whether Jewish or not. Human beings, however, do not change, and we all carry baggage from the past—much of which is "futile." *Futile* is a very good word because it perfectly summarizes a great deal of the way we traditionally think, behave, and react. These patterns of behavior are often pointless, sometimes downright stupid, and occasionally even farcical. And there seems to be very little we can, left to ourselves, do about these futile ways.

Recently my wife and I were involved in a fascinating and significant time on a retreat near Rome. We were studying the work of God in Simon Peter and eventually looked at this particular passage. One of the spiritual exercises we all followed was to go away on our own for an hour or more, in order to let God bring to mind any futile habits, attitudes, likes and dislikes, fears, reactions inherited from the past—from our parents or from others. We each wrote down a list (some were very long), mentioning as well any positive and productive influences from the past. At our service of Holy Communion on Thursday night, we each had the opportunity to place the lists on the Lord's table, as part of our prayers of confession. We then heard the Lord's forgiveness, and blotting out of the past, pronounced to us. These lists were then destroyed.

In the context of a service of Holy Communion, in which we vividly recollected in the bread and the wine the infinite cost of our redemption from these, and all, futile ways, this whole experience was extremely moving and liberating. Because each person's list was private and remained unread by others, I do not know what those futile ways in fifty people's lives amounted to. The next morning one of the group spoke about one such futile way.

When she was about eleven or twelve, she had begun to search seriously and questioningly for the reality of God. At her new school her headmistress encouraged anyone with queries to write them down on a piece of paper, so that in anonymity they could be used as material for services in the school chapel that term. This girl was prompted to ask a question about a matter of faith that profoundly worried her. At chapel soon after, her question was read by the headmistress, who then proceeded to misinterpret the question completely and to pour scorn on the ignorance and even presumptuousness of the person who could ask such a question.

Ever since, she had been totally unable to talk to anyone at any level about Christian faith and commitment. She has been scared stiff of getting it wrong and being made to look foolish. Since finding a personal faith in Christ only recently, over the age of forty, she has still been in bondage to that futile way inherited from her former headmistress. For the first time in thirty years, she believed, she realized that Jesus Christ had released her from the grip of the woman's behavior. How? Through His precious blood shed on the cross. The Holy Spirit had done, and was in the process of doing, what He delights to do—taking the words and the work of Jesus and making them come alive to us.

Now, as Peter himself goes on to say, she has "confidence in God, who raised [Jesus] from the dead and gave him glory, so that your faith and hope are in God" (1 Peter 1:21). To understand a little bit of how the death of Jesus two thousand years ago can release us today from such bondage from the past, we need to focus on Peter's remarkable statement in verse 20: "He was destined [as the Lamb of God] before the foundation of the world but was made manifest at the end of the times for your sake." God planned this redemption from eternity, and He executed His plan in history—at Calvary. From God's perspective, therefore, the atoning death of His Son deals with everything in our lives, however buried in the recesses of our past, and however much it has controlled us or ruined our lives since. There is nothing too powerful for God in Christ to release us from its bondage.

CHECKS AND BALANCES

Much of our ministry for healing will, in fact, be more long term than might so far have been indicated. This ongoing ministry calls for a varied, sensitive, and careful use of resources in the economy of God. Often there is a need for specific counseling, either from experienced Christians or from professional counselors, or from both. Part of the necessary wisdom lies in discovering which kind of resource is the most appropriate, and when it is best perhaps to place everything on hold and let things take their course. There is such a thing as overcounseling, both from the counselee's perspective in that receiving attention is almost like a drug and cannot be easily terminated, and from the counselor's perspective in that it is pleasant to be needed and difficult to let someone go. In either case, a situation of dependency can easily slip in unnoticed and unacknowledged.

For these reasons, among others, it is most advisable to establish some pattern of accountability and oversight among counselors in a local church. If there is in place a pattern of home groups, guidelines need to be drawn up covering expected procedures when an individual wants more than ordinary, reasonably spontaneous guidance. If the situation is likely to involve prolonged ministry, several points need to be taken into consideration. These are best dealt with in writing, for distribution to all home-group leaders and those involved in any counseling ministry in the congregation as a whole.

These points include the following questions: Has the person raised and discussed his or her needs with anyone else, inside or outside the home group, inside or outside the congregation? Is it possible to establish where that previous ministry was left and of what it consisted? Is there a tendency to "play the field" by moving from one person to another? Does the person actually want to be healed, or does he or she rather enjoy, or even find identity in, being sick? Is there anything in the person's background or lifestyle that might have created a loophole for demonic forces to penetrate? What is the reality and character of the person's relationship with God? Has the person clearly and with conviction surrendered his or her life to Jesus Christ as Lord? Does the person understand adequately the significance of the Cross? Has the person come to experience the power of the Holy Spirit in his or her life? Is there, as far as can be established, a genuine openness to God and a proper honesty both with the person and with the counselor? Is there a readiness to conform behavior to the pattern of discipleship set out in the Scriptures, and an acceptance of their authority for daily living?

These aspects, which with others can act as a checklist for counselors, are all focused on matters presented by the counselee. There is an equal need to cover certain key issues with counselors. It would be wrong to become too controlling and inflexible in a desire to avoid the inevitable pressures and problems in the ministry. Nevertheless, those entrusted with pastoral oversight have a responsibility to their people, which includes the obligation not to let wolves in sheep's clothing loose among the flock. Therefore, we are bound to have in place both training and supervision for all involved in the counseling ministry, with a senior member of staff (the pastor/minister if necessary and appropriate) personally acquainted with each individual concerned.

Training and supervision of counselors should be provided before any organized counseling begins, and should be regularly maintained in the life of the church. Counselors value the opportunity for regular debriefing, particularly if it is with a professionally trained clinical psychologist or psychiatrist from another local church.

There is great value, also, in "counseling-in-pairs." This is often a most effective way for those not particularly or professionally trained in counseling. It is also a good way to use one with considerable experience alongside another new to counseling. Provided the person being counseled is relaxed about this method, it can become an informal, inbuilt resource for checks and balances. The pair can brief and debrief together. It has proved extremely effective when it is understood that one of the two will concentrate on listening to the person being counseled, while the other concentrates on listening to the Holy Spirit. The roles may switch backward and forward during any one session or sessions.

Guidelines are necessary also, for practical matters such as the following: How long should one session last? Is it counterproductive to go beyond a certain length? Where is the best place for counseling? If several sessions are thought to be important, how many and how frequent should they be? What about men counseling women, and vice versa?

Due consideration and recognition must be given to areas of specialist counseling. It may be that a church possesses such skilled specialists within its own ranks. Otherwise, it is essential to know who is available and to establish the procedure for deciding when to call in these people. I am thinking of areas involving drug and alcohol abuse, child abuse, rape, abortion, marriage counseling, bereavement, and particular psychiatric conditions. There are others.

DELIVERANCE FROM DEMONIC FORCES

We have already touched, in previous chapters, on the ministry of deliverance from demonic forces. The commission and the authority to minister in this dimension was entrusted to the Church as a whole, not to specialists. But we still need to be wise as serpents in this, as in every, area of ministry. Any situation in which the demonic is likely to be present is best brought to, if not handled by, the ordained staff. They may well choose to include others, but it is dangerous to allow anyone to be involved except under authority. The major reason is actually spiritual, not pragmatic: the forces of darkness recognize duly constituted lines of authority in the Church of Jesus Christ, and experience demonstrates that the unwary and the inexperienced can hit real trouble.

WHOLENESS THROUGH SACRAMENTS

There is another aspect of the healing ministry of the local church where the role of the ordained person/people is significant. I have at times referred in passing to the sacramental ministry in general, and to anointing with oil in particular. It is worth explaining this in more detail. By sacramental ministry I am referring not just to the two sacraments of the gospel — baptism and the Lord's Supper — but to the different ways that the Lord seems to use symbols, actions, liturgical statements, and historically significant objects as channels of His grace in salvation. I am aware that this may be strange, if not suspicious, ground for some, and I will try to relieve some fears.

In general, the sacramental aspect of ministry is a healthy complement to prayer and counseling in a more informal context. Sacramental ministry is best carried out as follows: in a consecrated building, in a public but not embarrassingly exposed way, by those officially authorized by the wider church through ordination, using set prayers or forms of ministry, without any lengthy conversation or counseling, and in the context of congregational prayer and worship. In addition, such ministry seems most acceptable and effective when that worship is Eucharistic, that is, in the context of Holy Communion.

Those for whom any ministry of healing is strange will often find their way into an experience of greater wholeness through this kind of ministry. It is unthreatening, because it requires very little explanation or answering of questions on their part. It also "feels right" for those who have not been brought up in the rather free-and-easy atmosphere of many churches. It helps such people to move forward one stage from the anonymity and privacy of their traditional worship.

Holy Communion

This kind of sacramental ministry can begin in very simple ways. For me it started when we first used Christian names in administering bread and wine at Holy Communion. This habit—as it has now been for over twenty years—still hits people amidships when they first experience it. The private, very intimate act of receiving bread and wine becomes intensely personal: "He died for me."

Such a practice puts immense strain, of course, on the memory of the officiating minister. I have by now stopped being hopelessly embarrassed when I forget the name of one of the leaders with whom I meet weekly. It is certainly very hard, and may be invidious, to maintain this practice in a congregation of any size, because many will have their names forgotten and may feel excluded. Actually, our method of administration (which involves one person giving the bread and two the wine) means that most people will be known by one of the three. It is surprising, in spite of all the practical untidiness of this practice, how significant it has been in building truly Christian community life among the people of God. At this high point in the congregation's corporate worship the individual counts, matters, is known by name. That is part of the healing ministry of the local church.

It can actually be taken further in the act of receiving bread and wine. Along with my colleagues, who are often more bold and imaginative in the Spirit than myself, I sometimes use a brief prayer over an individual as well as regular words of administration from our liturgy. I might, as well, adapt those words to tie them in with either the theme of the service or the personal circumstances of the individual, couple, or family in front of me.

This can, however, take one into unfamiliar territory. One of my colleagues was administering the bread and came to a person known to him by name, but not intimately. He said, "John, eat this in remembrance that Jesus died for you, and may you see Him face to face." The man was very moved by these simple words, spoken to him and overheard by his wife kneeling beside him. On Tuesday, at the age of fifty-eight, he had a massive heart attack and died in his wife's arms. After the shock of bereavement had given way to the ache of aloneness, his wife found my colleague's words that Sunday an immense encouragement. With the benefit of hindsight, she could see that the Lord, knowing John's days on earth were coming to an end, inspired words aimed for the intimacy of his soul.

Anointing with Oil

Here it is worth saying a few more things about anointing with oil. Sadly, the traditional practice of the Roman Catholic Church, called "Extreme Unction," has left a fatalistic mark in the psyche and subculture of many people familiar only with folk religion. Anointing with oil is seen by such people to be only for the dying and indicates there is no hope left, except beyond the grave. It requires clear biblical teaching, taken home by the Spirit to the heart and understanding, to bring home the fact that this ministry is in anticipation of healing, is appropriate in any kind of sickness, is part of the proper ministry of the "elders of the church," and can be made available normally and naturally on a regular basis. We now do so at every main service of Holy Communion, which means at least once every Sunday. We find that many people come forward to receive this ministry, which we hold in a side chapel, to which they can move easily at the same time they leave their seats for bread and wine.

While, at present, we have ordained staff actually anointing people, we also have one other recognized lay leader praying in silence for the person. Apart from the principle of ministering in pairs, we have found that the one praying is often given insight into the person's situation that can then be shared later in an appropriate way—although, given the nature of this ministry, we do not deliberately seek out the person. The simplicity and the relative privacy of such sacramental ministry is of its essence. It places no burden of expectation on the person, except to come and ask.

We do, in fact, try to organize our resources so that prayer ministry in a more counseling mode is also available at the same time—in another part of the side chapel. This gives individuals the option of either having straightforward anointing with oil, or discussing the situation more fully with a couple of people before having prayer. Sometimes, when a person comes forward, they are not sure which they want to have, so there is a wise and sensitive person available gently to question and guide them to the appropriate ministry.

As well as anointing with oil, there is also laying-on of hands. This simply and movingly expresses through touch the hand of God and the "I am with you" support of the Christian fellowship. Following New Testament examples, we use this sacramental ministry to signify a number of different things—being filled with the Spirit, being commissioned for specific service, being sent out from our church to another or for special ministry, being assured of the presence of the Lord to heal, and generally to bring assurance of the good hand of the Lord upon a person. In this latter sense the ministry is one in which a whole home group, gathered around one of its members, will express oneness and identification in need, distress, or sickness.

This example brings us back to every-member ministry and the openness of every Christian to give and receive in the healing community of the local church. Jesus is the One who heals: the Holy Spirit is the true Counselor. Through the death of Jesus on the cross, where "he took our infirmities and bore our diseases" (Matthew 8:17), we have been made heirs of all the fullness of the Kingdom of God, with all its comprehensive blessings. Matthew quotes Isaiah 53 to explain the basis on which healing, such as Peter's mother-in-law being freed from a fever and a centurion's servant from paralysis (as well as general healing and demonic deliverance; see Matthew 8:5-16), has been made available.

In that remarkable chapter, presaging the Suffering Servant's atoning death for our sins and our sicknesses, the full scope of our salvation was gloriously outlined. Jesus has fleshed out the prophecy. Whatever blessing we now enjoy comes as the fruit of His atonement at Calvary, whether it is forgiveness and cleansing from all sin, deliverance from the forces of darkness, power to lead a holy life, guidance on our daily path, or healing from sickness and infirmity. Each and every one of these good things comes from our gracious God, who did not spare His own Son but gave Him up for us all, not withholding anything from us in giving us His Son.

1. What reactions do you have to "the healing ministry" in the context of your local church?

2. In what practical ways can healing effectively and sensitively develop as a part of your church's ministry?

3. Is there a need for the overall counseling ministry in your church to be reevaluated and better coordinated? Explain.

4. Is there a place in your church for using more fully the sacramental aspects of a healing ministry? Why do you feel that way?

5. "Jesus is the One who heals: the Holy Spirit is the true Counselor" — how can this emphasis be underlined in your church?

CHAPTER EIGHT

FACING THE PROBLEMS

I t is time to look directly at the way we tackle the problems of local church life and, even more, at the attitudes we take and pass on about suffering. And it is only proper that we do this immediately after considering the healing ministry of the local church. That ministry will find authentic expression *only* in the context of a Christian community that has learned, not just how to suffer and cope with suffering in their midst and all around them, but how to share in Christ's sufferings "for the sake of his body, that is, the church" — as the Apostle Paul enigmatically wrote (Colossians 1:24).

THE HUMDRUM

We will begin quite a long way back from where we hope to arrive — with "the incessant drumming of the humdrum," to use playwright Christopher Fry's evocative phrase. This is the beat to which we all march for most of our lives. The humdrum is everyday living, the routine, the basics that are always there and simply have to be done. For some the humdrum of the routine is safe and sound; they want nothing else and nothing more. Most of us, however, want some breaks in the same old routine — if only to stop us from falling asleep bored to tears. There are a few people who cannot live without excitement upon excitement: they are forever looking for something to break the monotony, indeed, to prevent the monotony getting there in the first place.

The fact is, the humdrum is monotonous. A drum can produce only one tone. It is pointless wishing it were otherwise: pigs might fly first. Now, it seems to me that much local church life is the incessant drumming of the humdrum. The work of Christian ministry and the task of building Christian community life is, frankly, tedious. It all takes time and toil. Paul, for one, readily admitted as much. He called it by its proper name—labor, spending and being spent, agony and energy in equal measure (see 1 Corinthians 15:58, 2 Corinthians 12:15, Colossians 1:29). Much, if not most, of it is unglamorous and unspectacular: it is also largely unseen and, to that extent, unknown.

Confronting the Unavoidable

Those of us who know God's call to be involved full time in resourcing the community life of the Christian church do others no kind of service if we tell them otherwise or give them any other impression. Much disillusionment, first with local church life and then with Christian discipleship, has its roots in overromanticized accounts of what following Christ and His people is all about.

In the fundamental reorganization of our church here in London, about forty people have moved into overall leadership in the three congregations. Most of them had only guessed at what might be involved in running a church. Virtually all of them have full-time occupations; so their time is very limited—a factor we are trying to keep uppermost in developing new patterns of ministry and more people for ministry. After four or five weeks on the job, following two months of thorough preparation, the overriding impression gained by the three teams can be summarized in the comment "I never realized it took so much time sorting out all the details and the nitty-gritty of running a congregation."

When we were originally discussing the makeup of the three teams and then exploring the portfolios of each person and their job descriptions, it became obvious—on paper—that the work would be largely tedious and unexciting. But that was only on paper—now it is starting to bite. I am actually impressed with the application, the good humor, the imagination, and the sensitivity with which this ministry is being undertaken. These are early days, but the signs are encouraging.

This "thorns and thistles . . . sweat and dust" reality in all work since the ejection of Adam and Eve from paradise (see Genesis 3:17-19) is endemic to Christian ministry as well as secular work. There is one redeeming feature—in the full sense of the word. Paul makes this clear when he urges Christians in the decidedly difficult church of Corinth: "Be steadfast, immovable, always abounding in the work of the Lord, knowing that in the Lord your labor is not in vain" (or empty, pointless, useless; 1 Corinthians 15:58). It is extremely encouraging to know that trivial routine can be redeemed into work of eternal significance, if it is "in the Lord," that is, in His name, for His glory, by His strength, and with His people.

It seems to me that all the Lord's work is based on this very ordinary, hard labor—preaching, prayer, worship, teaching, evangelism, pastoral care, administration, healing, hospitality, helmsmanship, giving, helping, prophesying. Unless the basics are done well the ministry cannot thrive—and the basics are not done just once; they have to be continuously and consistently kept up.

Resisting Disillusionment

It must be apparent that we live in a culture that, by and large, is not much enamored with seemingly pointless, repetitive tasks. It is also a culture that wants instant gratification—without hassle, delay, or effort: an instant get-now-pay-later generation. Much of this is due to technology, which has taken routine tasks away from human beings and entrusted them to machines, especially to computers.

It must be right for a local church, whatever the size and scope of its ministry, to make the fullest possible use of modern equipment: indeed, it is irresponsible stewardship not to do so. We can genuinely thank God for taking some of the soul-destroying grind out of everyday work, Christian and secular, by means of modern technology.

This matter is, in brief, another example of allowing proper expectations to guide us in local church life. We have seen already the kind of disillusionment that can set in when people begin with false expectations of what lies in store in Christian discipleship. We can take the theme one step further by asserting that the problems, pressures, disappointments, and difficulties come thick and fast in a local church that is on the move. The problems of life are always preferable to the problems of death, but they are still large and heavy.

DISPELLING COMMON MISCONCEPTIONS

Several misconceptions need to be nailed at this point. First, there seems to be a belief that Christians will not let you down, will always keep their word, will go the extra mile, will be completely honest, will not gossip or break confidences. Yes, we expect unbelievers to behave in an unChristlike way; but somehow it has become accepted that you can always trust Christians to be, well, perfect. We simply have to put this misconception into words to know how ridiculous it is. And yet scores of people in local churches up and down the land have become jaundiced and cynical in their discipleship, because "Christians do not come up to my expectations." In some way we need to discover how to become realistic about and with one another, without accepting the lowest common denominator for our walk together with the Lord.

A second misconception is that problems and difficulties indicate that we have missed God's way, and may even be just recompense for our disobedience and lack of faith. If, instead, we expect to meet problems and difficulties in following, or trying honestly to follow, the way God seems to be indicating, we can tackle them in the right spirit. One golden rule here is to meet them, not pretend to have not noticed them or, even more, that they are not there. Putting off finding a solution invariably increases the size and the complexity of the problem.

A third misconception is that problems are resolved by prayer and by more prayer, that the problems will go away as we pray—and if they do not go away it is because we are not praying enough or our prayer is deficient. Prayer, however central and crucial, is no substitute for both tackling the problem and getting alongside people involved in the problems. There are no problems without people. Perhaps the root of this particular misconception lies as much in a utilitarian attitude to prayer, which sees its value in its results, as in a naive and overspiritual attitude to personal relationships.

A fourth misconception is the scapegoat syndrome— that is, the approach to problems that invariably looks for the one who is causing all the trouble, in the belief that sorting that person out will sort out the problem. Rarely is this the reason for the problem in a church; it is a breakdown in communication, as often as not, with no wilfulness or individual blame to be attached to any one person. The fact is that things go wrong and people get the short end of the stick.

A fifth misconception is a simplistic belief that Satan is responsible for all the problems and that, if only we took the authority of Jesus Christ over the devices of the Enemy, everything would come out right. As we will consider more fully in a moment, it is also naive to disregard or discount the role Satan does play in the life of any local church; but we must neither credit him with what he has not done nor ignore the way our very human spirits (not evil spirits) cause problems for us all.

THE DEVIL'S FINGERPRINT

In what ways, then, does Satan go to work in a church? We cannot identify the methods or the actions of Satan apart from what Scriptures tell us. To do otherwise is truly to walk in the darkness of our own imaginings—something he would certainly like us to do. Paul, writing to a local church with which he had the closest ties and frequent contact—that is, Corinth—said plainly of Satan: "We are not ignorant of his designs" (2 Corinthians 2:11), or "we are not unaware of his schemes" (NIV). It will be valuable, therefore, to trace the apostle's experienced knowledge of the way Satan operates, especially in Paul's correspondence with the Corinthians. This is particularly valuable because these letters, of all the documents in the New Testament, address problems in a local church. It is important, for that reason, to note the areas where Paul does *not* detect Satan's involvement, as much as those where he does.

First Corinthians
The first four chapters of 1 Corinthians cover issues in the church such as division based on allegiance to personalities, the message of the Cross, the choice of individuals by God to respond to His call, the preaching of the gospel at Corinth, the work of the Spirit in revealing God's wisdom, the emptiness and deceptiveness of human wisdom, the fact of answerability to God, the pressure of arrogant warpers of the truth in the church at Corinth. In none of these does Satan merit a mention.

Chapter 5 describes a person living in unprecedented immorality, but allowed to continue as a fully communicant member of the local church. Paul is appalled by the Corinthians' complacency and arrogance and instructs them to act "with the power of the Lord Jesus . . . to deliver this man to Satan for the destruction of the flesh, that his spirit may be saved in the day of the Lord Jesus" (5:4-5). Satan has power to destroy an individual's flesh (that is, terminate his or her physical life) — *but* only if and when the Lord Jesus, for His own purposes, gives him such power.

In chapter 7, Paul gives extremely wise practical advice to individuals and to couples who are thinking about marriage, either in prospect or from the inside. In particular, he counsels married couples to enjoy the gift of their sexuality uninhibitedly, each giving themselves to the other without reservation — except when God calls them to a special time of prayer. Even then they must resume sexual relations after a while, "lest Satan tempt you through lack of self-control" (7:5). In other words, one of Satan's methods in a church is to break up Christian marriages by tempting either or both partners into unfaithfulness — and he chooses times of strong spirituality and intensive prayer to strike. This is an important corrective to old adages like "the family that prays together stays together": if taken too seriously, such a piece of advice induces complacency at precisely the time of maximum vulnerability.

Chapter 10 describes the incongruity, indeed the impossibility, of Christians taking part in worship that is offered, in whatever form, to idols, or to gods other than the God and Father of our Lord Jesus Christ. To do so, says Paul, is "to be partners with demons." No wonder he states that "you cannot partake of the table of the Lord and the table of demons" (10:21). So much for any talk of interfaith services of prayer.

In the intervening chapters (8 and 9) Paul addresses a number of issues related to the idolatrous, pagan culture in which the church at Corinth lived out its discipleship. At every point he exhorts them to wholehearted commitment to Jesus as Lord — a theme he continues in chapters 12–14, where he tackles the proper expression of spiritual gifts in the local church. In all this treatment he does not mention the influence of Satan; nor does he in talking in such vivid and compelling terms about the resurrection of Jesus and the resurrection of those who belong to Jesus (chapter 15). This remains true even when Paul writes about the end of all things, the moment when time ends and God is "everything to every one" (15:28). All the enemies of God have then been put under the feet of Jesus, but even at that point no explicit mention is made of Satan. "The last enemy" is death.

Second Corinthians

When we move to 2 Corinthians, the references to Satan are equally important and fascinating. When Paul emphasizes his personal knowledge of Satan's designs, devices, and schemes, he is writing in the context of a particular series of broken relationships (2:11). He strongly stresses his forgiveness of anyone who might have caused offense to him or any Christian at Corinth. He is insistent and plain about this forgiveness on his part, because he is well aware of Satan's ploy in keeping Christians divided. If he cannot actually down a Christian, he will do all he can to divide brother from brother, sister from sister. That method we certainly need to watch out for and counter.

In 4:4 Paul provides a vital perspective on the challenge and realities of evangelism. He explains that "the god of this world has blinded the minds of the unbelievers, to keep them from seeing the light of the gospel of the glory of Christ, who is the likeness of God." It is crucial to take Paul's insights with utter seriousness in our evangelistic endeavors as a local church. If Satan is at work causing such intellectual darkness, we must plan our campaign accordingly. More of that in the next chapter.

As he proceeds with this letter, Paul bares his soul in an unprecedented manner. He talks openly of his own agony and pressures in ministry in moving terms. He describes his persecutions, his hardships, his afflictions in the most vivid way—but he does not once mention Satan (4:7-12, 6:4-10). This is surely significant, and we will return to it later.

The next mention of Satan is in 6:14 when the apostle

once again pleads for distinctive holiness from Christians in the face of a multicultural and idolatrous culture: do not compromise, do not mix the two, do not try to have the best of both worlds; be clear for Christ, because Christ and Belial (Satan) have nothing at all in common. Satan never tires of luring disciples of Jesus to compromise their loyalty—not least in the partnerships and matings we enter into.

When Paul moves on to respond to personal attacks on his own ministry and calling as an apostle, he can scarcely restrain himself—although he realizes he should (see chapters 11–12). He is clear that one of Satan's original ploys was to lead God's children away from "a sincere and pure devotion to Christ" (11:3) by subtle and persuasive versions of the gospel, which are not gospel/good news at all. In those and similar ways, by using especially "deceitful workmen," Satan goes about unrecognized in local churches, disguising himself "as an angel of light" (11:13-14). Satan does nothing outrageous, nothing too objectionable, nothing too obvious; he simply muddies the waters and confuses the minds of ordinary believers with intellectually sophisticated ideas about the nature, mission, ministry, death, resurrection, and return of Jesus. Satan's deception still operates in these areas today, sowing doubt about the straightforward truth of the gospel.

Paul's final reference to Satan in his correspondence with the church at Corinth brings them and us full circle. He talks of his "thorn in the flesh," which three times he pleaded with God to remove, but each time received the clear reply "No." Paul became aware that this thorn in the flesh was specifically sent by God to keep him humble, dependent on God, able to learn in experience the secret of all ministry—that God's power is made perfect in our weaknesses (12:9). As with the apostle's declaration about the blatantly immoral Christian mentioned in 1 Corinthians 5, so here Paul's bodily condition was, by God's ordination, part of Satan's permitted influence. Paul calls his thorn in the flesh "a messenger of Satan" (12:7). So, physical weakness in disciples of Jesus can be *both* the gift of God *and* the messenger of Satan.

Conclusions

From Paul's letters to the church at Corinth, therefore, we have penetrating and significant insights into the devices of Satan in any local church. He has no new tricks and no unrevealed methods. Jesus Himself exposed all Satan's ploys and stratagems, both in His three years of public ministry and, supremely, in His three hours of public agony on the cross. Satan has no more cards to play; he has played his ace in seeing to the execution of Jesus — the death of God, or so he thought. But God trumped the Devil's ace by resurrection. We share with Jesus in this resurrection life. In Him we can celebrate victory over all the wiles of the Devil.

But it means using the right weapons. As Paul told the church at Corinth, "For though we live in the world we are not carrying on a worldly war, for the weapons of our warfare are not worldly but have divine power to destroy strongholds" (2 Corinthians 10:3-4). In Ephesians 6:11 Paul is more explicit about these weapons, calling them "the whole armor of God." It is plain that Paul lived daily in the conscious reality of this spiritual battle. The details of this teaching on God's armor make this emphatically clear, not least in the specific tenses of the verbs he uses.

The first three pieces of armor are never to be taken off. The Roman soldier, after whom Paul is modeling his instructions here, in a battle situation never marched or slept without his breastplate, girdle, and sandals. When the trumpet sounded to engage the enemy, he donned his helmet and took up his sword and shield. Paul tells us as Christian soldiers to stand against the enemy "*having* girded your loins with truth, and *having* put on the breastplate of righteousness, and *having* shod your feet with the equipment of the gospel of peace" (6:13-14, emphasis added). We can never afford to be without these three—truth in the inward being, clothed in the righteousness of Christ, and always ready to proclaim the good news of peace through Jesus.

But, in any situation, Christian believers must be instantly alert to seize the Word of God, to put on God's salvation and to move out in faith together to pull down enemy strongholds and smash the very gates of hell. The shield of a Roman soldier had a rim by which he interlocked with his comrades. They then advanced together with locked shields in attacking a city. The array of locked shields was perfect protection against fiery arrows and flaming pitch launched at them from city ramparts. From above, the shields looked like a tortoise shell and the Romans called this formation exactly that—*testudo*. Interlocked with each other, we move against the strongholds of Satan in faith, faith in the God of battles who has overcome by the blood of the Lamb.

We can see, hopefully, how essential it is to be alert and vigilant in face of the devices, the old and familiar devices, of Satan in his bitter hatred of the Church of Jesus Christ. It is not surprising that those disciples who take Jesus seriously encounter real opposition. Although it is not accurate to attribute problems and difficulties to Satan, it is clearly important to ask the Lord to give us discernment about Satan's influence in the life of the church—and to act accordingly.

The old farmer at the bottom of the hill here in the Pyrenees was part of the French Resistance during the Second World War. He regularly hid Allied soldiers on the run in and around the farm. At the right time they would be directed across the mountains to Spain—a fast eight-hour trek to freedom done under cover of night. This valley was, in fact, one of only three such escape routes in this part of the world.

As soldiers of Christ we are in God's Resistance in enemy-held territory. Our task is to see people to freedom. The Enemy has invaded territory that does not belong to him, and we know that one day he will finally be put down and eliminated. Till then we are to be vigilant, resisting him whenever he gets up to his, by now, predictable devices. Sometimes he comes to us like a roaring lion, seeking someone to devour (1 Peter 5:8); at others, he comes disguised as an angel of light, all smarm and charm, with a smile on his face, trying to wheedle us into his way of thinking and into maintaining his will in our part of God's world. However he treats us, we must resist him — which means recognizing his presence and methods, exposing them for all to see, renouncing any influence he is trying to exercise . . . and declaring together that our allegiance is to Jesus Christ as Lord. We have the promise of Scripture: "Resist the devil and he will flee from you. Draw near to God and he will draw near to you" (James 4:7-8).

This contrast is the difference between Satan and God. Satan does not like close encounters, God speaks and acts in truth. Satan plays on fears, God wins us by His love. Satan is determined to destroy, God is committed to building and creating. Satan likes secrecy, God chooses openness. Satan rules by dividing, God stoops to conquer by serving. Satan pulls people apart, God gathers people together. This essential contrast between "the god of this world" and the God "who so loved the world" can act as an instructive litmus test in all church life: neither Satan nor God can act out of character, and the footprints of each are normally recognizable.

THE GIFT OF SUFFERING

Enough of Satan. The final perspective on the trials and pressures of church life in this chapter must major on one of two primary gifts of God. Paul describes these two gifts in his letter to the church at Philippi, a letter he wrote from prison — so many good things seem to come from Christians in prison. This is how he puts it: "It has been granted to you that for the sake of Christ you should not only believe in him but also suffer for his sake, engaged in the same conflict which you saw and now hear to be mine" (1:29-30).

Grace

The Greek word translated "was granted" literally means "was graced": the root word is *charis*. Faith in Jesus as Lord we know well to be God's grace, a gift we do not deserve and cannot earn. Suffering for the sake of Jesus is also God's grace, a gift we do not deserve and cannot earn. Paul is very plain about this—it is equally a privilege to believe in Christ and to suffer for Christ. The "conflict" he then mentions, or "agony" (the Greek word originally refers to a contest in the athletic games or any highly competitive and demanding arena), was something well known to the local church at Philippi. They had first seen Paul experiencing it; now they had heard that he was experiencing it again. The difference was that they too were apparently in the thick of it themselves.

Can we be more precise about the nature of this conflict, this agonizing struggle or contest? If it is a gift of God's grace, presented both to the apostle and to this local church, it is important to identify it so that we can recognize the gift when God grants us the same privilege.

The Real Conflict

At first sight it is tempting to assume that Paul's conflict was what he describes a few times "as my imprisonment" (1:7,13-14,17). Paul's time at Philippi, described in Acts 16, had culminated in a night in prison, after being falsely accused with Silas of disturbing the peace. They were seized, dragged, attacked, stripped, beaten, imprisoned, and chained. Now, as he writes this letter to the Philippians, he is in prison again. He stresses, moreover, that they had first *seen* his conflict and were now *hearing* about it. They could have seen it only when he was actually at Philippi.

Taking a closer look, however, we have to draw a different conclusion. Paul has just talked about "your opponents" (1:28), literally "those set against you," and calls this experience of theirs "the same conflict" (1:30) as his own original conflict at Philippi and his present conflict. It is never prudent to argue fully and finally from silence, but there is no record of Christians in the church at Philippi being actually thrown into prison at the same time as this letter was being written—certainly not in any widespread sense that would have led Paul to say the church as a whole was facing, let alone experiencing, imprisonment for the gospel.

The strongest argument comes, in fact, in the text of Philippians. In chapter 3, Paul talks about that transforming experience, dramatically brought about on the road to Damascus but relived in the conscious decisiveness of each day since, which led him to count all things like so much trash in order that he might find Christ and be found in Christ. That single-minded determination daily introduced him to two realities: the power of Christ's resurrection and the fellowship of Christ's sufferings. He knew the impact of both in his life and in his ministry. One thing gripped him: to press on each new day in knowing Christ more and more in these two ways; never to relax or to look back at past progress or past failure, but to refuse rest and to know dissatisfaction until he had claimed for his own that for which Christ had claimed him all those years ago—"the prize of the upward call of God in Christ Jesus."

This is what drove Paul onward and upward. It was a demanding and formidable vision. It was, within its very nature, a conflict and an agony—power and suffering mixed together. It was the way of Christ and therefore it must be the way of His apostle. It must also be the way for every disciple of Christ and every church of Christ. That was Paul's passionate conviction. Resurrection comes out of the cross and leads to the way of the cross.

But there were people at Philippi, at Ephesus, at Thessalonica, at Rome, at Corinth—all of them members of the local church—who thought and acted differently. They lived within the believing community, they took part in worship and fellowship; but they lived their daily lives as "enemies of the cross of Christ" (3:18). Paul's eyes filled with tears whenever he thought about them, because he knew many of them well. They had come to Christ through his preaching and his personal work. He could see their faces and remember their stories as he was dictating this letter—"Their god is the belly . . . with minds set on earthly things." They rejected the way of the cross.

That was where the conflict came—for Paul and for the church at Philippi. That is what caused the agony—these halfhearted, backsliding disciples who opposed any wholehearted, forward-moving plan for the church. They were the bitterest opponents of Paul and all that he stood for. They had so set their minds on earthly things, that ruling one's life by "the prize" in Heaven was quietly—and sometimes bluntly—ridiculed. The blessings of God are for now, they said; God wants His children to be rich, prosperous "kings." Paul had faced that opposition and conflict before, particularly at Corinth, and now it had reared its head again at Philippi. It has also reared its head defiantly in the last twenty to thirty years in the churches of the West, spreading its tentacles to imprison some church leaders in Africa and Latin America. They reject the way of the cross.

Avoiding the Gift

There had actually been signs from the earliest days of the church at Philippi. Paul had been plagued, going about his daily work and ministry, by a demonized slave girl who had a spirit of divination. This facility brought her owners a lucrative income, as she predicted the future by her occult gift. She used to follow Paul and Silas around the streets, screaming out "These men are servants of the

Most High God, who proclaim to you the way of salvation"
(Acts 16:17). When Paul commanded the unclean spirit to
leave in the name of Jesus Christ, the spirit left the girl — and
her owners realized very soon that "their hope of gain" had
also left (Luke uses exactly the same word, literally "went
away"). They then caused the mayhem that resulted in Paul
and Silas being imprisoned. "Hope of gain" lies deep in the
human heart; love of money is the root of all evils, and it
does not leave Christians, at Philippi or anywhere else, on
conversion.

The gracious gift of God to all believers of knowing
the fellowship of Christ's sufferings is an unwelcome privilege for those who think that "godliness is a means of
gain" (1 Timothy 6:5). Such members of any local church
will always fight against an emphasis on suffering. Paul's
clearest words on the subject are, in fact, written to young
Timothy, bishop of Ephesus — "Share in suffering as a good
soldier of Christ Jesus" (2 Timothy 2:3); "Share in suffering
for the gospel in the power of God" (1:8); "For this gospel
I was appointed a preacher and apostle and teacher, and
therefore I suffer as I do" (1:11-12); "As for you, always
be steady, endure suffering" (4:5); "You have observed my
teaching, my conduct, my aim in life, my faith, my patience,
my love, my steadfastness, my persecutions, my sufferings. . . . Indeed all who desire to live a godly life in Christ
Jesus will be persecuted" (3:10-12).

Paul also tells Timothy plainly that the true gospel and
the full implications of discipleship will come under special
assault "in the last days" (3:1). These times of "stress" will
be characterized by people whose love is not for God or
for Jesus Christ, but they will be "lovers of self, lovers of
money, . . . lovers of pleasure rather than lovers of God."
Yes, they will hold "the form of religion," but they will deny
"the power of it." The force of their denial is that they do
not see the point of power to change lives to become like
Jesus Christ, because they see religion as giving them power

to live the way they want to live, not to walk the way of the cross.

These men operate in particular ways: "Among them are those who make their way into households and capture weak women, burdened with sins and swayed by various impulses, who will listen to anybody and can never arrive at a knowledge of the truth." There have been such smooth operators in every generation. Moses had to cope with Jannes and Jambres, who apparently used the magic arts to work their own way into people's homes and hearts. In Paul's day, it was probably straightforward visiting in homes, targeting vulnerable women in the Christian community. Today, they come in pairs dressed in smart suits and promising security and happiness. They also come into people's homes via television and radio, targeting those disillusioned with formal churchgoing and peddling a version of discipleship that cuts out commitment, in any Christ-honoring way, to a local church.

Not all the opponents of authentic Christianity operate like this; it is only "among them" that this particular approach is taken. Others operate in other ways. Paul ends his second letter to Timothy (the last one he wrote, as far as we know, and also written in prison) by mentioning the names of two people who had caused him much pain (4:10,14). The first is Demas who, "in love with this present world," had deserted Paul—the world attracted Demas more than the cross.

The second is Alexander the coppersmith. The church at Ephesus had from the outset been opposed to the wealthy and the influential trade guilds in the city (Acts 19:23-27). First, it was the silversmiths who lived in luxury on the proceeds of their silver statuettes of the goddess Artemis. They saw their whole standard of living plummeting, if these idols were no longer used by Ephesians (and many visitors and merchants) who turned seriously to Christ.

Was Alexander the leader of the guild of coppersmiths at Ephesus? Is he the Alexander mentioned by Luke (Acts

19:33-34), a Jew who was prepared to defend Paul at this early stage? After he became a disciple, did he begin to feel pressure from other silversmiths? Did he cause Paul great harm by undermining or even contradicting his call to holiness and wholehearted discipleship?

We cannot be one hundred percent sure about these details, but the general thrust of the biblical record is unmistakable. The clear message about the nature of conflict, in Paul and in every true disciple of Christ, gains meaning by its very topical relevance to the problems facing us today. The local church at Philippi opted, in the majority, for the prize of "the upward call of God in Christ Jesus." Many chose to live differently "as enemies of the cross of Christ." What about our church? Where do the majority stand on the double privilege of believing and suffering? What about those who oppose this emphasis and any plans to conform church life, let alone their own personal lives, to the pattern of Jesus? The inner conflict of our double calling (to faith and to suffering, to know the power of Christ's resurrection and the fellowship of His sufferings) will never fade this side of Heaven. The more public conflict with those opposed to such a calling will also never go away, and the existence of such people in and around our church will intensify our inner conflict for them, as well as our own agony with our true calling. For us—as for Paul—the tears will not cease.

The Importance of Death

These tears represent one fundamental truth of all authentic ministry: If a person or a couple or a group or a church is to discover true life, then somebody somewhere must experience death. Paul spelled that out to the triumphal church at Corinth, who never chose to walk the way of the cross if they could help it. Writing about "the treasure" of the gospel and the glorious ministry of the Spirit in the New Covenant, he says: "We have this treasure in earthen vessels. . . . We are afflicted in every way . . . perplexed, . . .

persecuted, . . . struck down . . . ; always carrying in the body the death of Jesus, so that the life of Jesus may also be manifested in our bodies. For while we live we are always being given up to death for Jesus' sake, so that the life of Jesus may be manifested in our mortal flesh. So death is at work in us, but life in you" (2 Corinthians 4:7-12).

This is the costly way that "grace extends to more and more people" (4:15), and so God is glorified, because it is obvious from this truth that "the transcendent power belongs to God and not to us" (4:7). As, therefore, we choose to embrace our weakness, to enter thus into the fellowship of Christ's sufferings, to do so on behalf of His Body the Church, so our community life will come to know the working of His Holy Spirit in truly transcendent power.

*   *   *

1. To what extent do people in your church show commitment to the long haul and the routine chores of Christian discipleship?

2. Do you think people in your church are realistic or overspiritual about the everyday problems and hassles of church life?

3. Where can you see Satan's fingerprints in your local church's life?

4. Do you see evidence in your church of the conflict between those who accept the call to walk the way of the cross and those who see Christian faith as a way to success and happiness? What do you see?

5. In what ways is God calling you to experience "death," so that others can find life?

CHAPTER NINE

TURNING INSIDE OUT

G od's primary unit for evangelization is the local church. Our reaction to that statement will depend on a number of things. Some will instinctively feel like saying, "Yes, and that's why evangelism isn't going very far." Others will already have decided that God's primary unit lies elsewhere, probably among those committed to evangelization, and that their evangelistic energies will—for the time being at least—be channeled accordingly. There will be those who find a warmer response in their hearts, because they are beginning to see the truth of it in practice, not just in theory.

In strictly historical terms, looking at the last fifty years or so, the conviction stated at the beginning of this chapter has emerged very gradually and almost reluctantly. This period began with the birth of many evangelistic initiatives, especially aimed at children, teenagers, university and college students—at young people in general. The widespread success of these ministries, in bringing people to faith, motivated other specialized ventures—in prisons, in the armed forces, in business and industry, in politics, in different professions. In some cases, individuals had already been involved in pioneering work, but concerted initiatives began to become notably influential from the 1960s onward.

These trends were reflected in, for example, the congress on world evangelism held in Lausanne, Switzerland, in 1974. The main contributors—and probably the bulk of those attending—were from these evangelistic agencies, missions, and movements. In the Lausanne Covenant there was, it should be noted, no mention of the local church.

Only in the last twenty years has the primary role of the local church become widely accepted and reinstated in strategies for evangelism. This has been brought about both by a more thorough biblical theology, and by the reawakening or the emergence of local churches that truly are units for evangelization. Lausanne II, held in Manila in 1989, produced a manifesto that reflects this switch in emphasis. One of its twenty-one affirmations explicitly states: "We affirm that every Christian congregation must turn itself outwards to its local community in evangelistic witness and compassionate service."

Later in the manifesto, the compilers elaborate: "We believe that the local church bears a primary responsibility for the spread of the gospel." Noting that the Apostle Paul's letter to the church at Thessalonica refers to the fact that the gospel "came to you" and "sounded forth from you" (1 Thessalonians 1:5,8), the document continues: "Each local church must evangelise the district in which it is situated, and has the resources to do so." This section concludes: "We deeply regret that many of our congregations are inward-looking, organized for maintenance rather than mission, or preoccupied with church-based activities at the expense of witness. We determine to turn our churches inside out, so that they may engage in continuous outreach. . . ."

About the same time as Lausanne II, but unconnected with it, the bishop of Norwich, in the eastern part of England, issued a powerful challenge to his diocesan synod, in the light of the call from the 1988 Lambeth Conference of Anglican Bishops around the world to make the 1990s a decade of evangelism. His three main points for the diocese were the need to move from maintenance to mission, from clergy to laity, and from central to local control. Most of the mainline denominations, including the Roman Catholic Church, have declared the 1990s to be particularly devoted to evangelization.

We are, then, in good company in wanting to turn our church inside out, a revolution that is probably more constructive than turning it upside down—unless by that we mean those at the top learning to serve. In 1990 I was asked to address a follow-up meeting in Stuttgart for German leaders who wanted to take the Manila Manifesto further in their local areas throughout Germany. My specific topic was "Evangelism in the City Centre," and the bulk of this chapter is taken up with the main points I stressed on that occasion. There were, in fact, ten points, three of which I have already covered in earlier chapters. In Stuttgart I entitled them "Invest in Small Groups," "Pray for the Worship Services," and "Major on Shared Leadership." Here are the other seven.

INVESTIGATE THE SOCIAL CONDITIONS

First, *investigate the social conditions* of the neighborhood in which your church is located. Surprisingly, we can often think we know our community well, especially if we have lived there for some time, but closer investigation reveals how superficial our knowledge actually is.

It is always valuable to look at facts and figures, statistics and population, rather than draw rough and ready conclusions. This kind of information is normally obtainable from the local authorities.

Touring the neighborhood, on foot or in a car, is another important way of catching the feel of an area and of meeting people we would not normally encounter. The more leisurely pace involved in walking allows us to notice and absorb what we would otherwise miss completely.

The church is particularly responsible to be aware of and available to those in need in our community. Here, the local welfare and social agencies will be of limited use, although they certainly ought to be consulted and encouraged. Far more important are those who are ignored or missed by any system or network, those who live on their own, the housebound, the socially ignored or unacceptable.

Until we undertake this kind of research, we can fail to see what is staring us in the face. For example, I remember in Cape Town I had never appreciated the way apartheid policies (now thankfully being officially discarded) had divided families in that part of South Africa in a most devastating way. The largest grouping, talking racial classification terminology, in the Cape are the so-called Cape Colored people. Blacks and whites are both minorities.

When the National Party government came to power in 1948, they began a strategy of enforced classification by racial criteria of all in the country. The first criterion was physical appearance, the second was social association, the third (if neither of the above determined a person's classification) was the choice of the person as to which group he or she wanted to join. For the Cape Colored people this was a very painful time. Some were clearly dark-skinned and therefore assigned to the Cape Colored group. Others, however, were as fair-skinned as any white person but were also duly assigned there.

Those who were in between had to choose. This meant a choice between being "privileged" and without family, or being deprived and oppressed but staying with kith and kin. In our parish we had children of the same parents, one of whom had been classified colored and another who had opted to be white. The pain, the bitterness, the guilt, the fear can only be imagined.

Once I had registered this traumatic social and family reality, I found I had a very different perspective on both pastoral work and on evangelism. If the gospel is at heart a message of reconciliation, there was more to Christian ministry than recognizing the evils of apartheid, challenging it structurally, and showing Christ's better way. It must include working and praying for profound reconciliation in such situations, so that the local church truly began to flesh out another answer altogether.

Similarly, when we had been in central London for several months, I remember the jolt it gave me to appreciate that right there, at the heart of the nation and surrounded by thousands of commuters and tourists, over six thousand teenagers went to local schools — all within a ten-to-fifteen-minute walk of the church building. This fact *had* to be relevant in turning the congregation inside out.

The church we had served in Oxford was also in the city center. The traditional perception and description of Oxford is "town and gown," that is, city and university, workers and students. Although they walk past one another and mingle briefly every day of the week, only when we looked and listened more closely did we realize the potential explosiveness of this close proximity between the socially frustrated young people of the city and the specially privileged students.

Perhaps one of the first aims, therefore, of such an investigation is to listen — to listen to the actual cries of the human heart, especially those who have no link with the church or with God. We cannot begin to reach them where they are, unless we have heard them properly.

UNDERSTAND THE RELIGIOUS ATMOSPHERE

Our second priority, in turning the church inside out, is to *understand the religious atmosphere*. The world of the 1990s is, in this sense, a fascinating and somewhat daunting place, particularly in the West. In the last four decades the mood has changed in an intriguing way.

The fifties were years of rebuilding after the Second World War, serious with a sense of responsibility toward those who had put their lives on the line for freedom. The

sixties marked a transition to unprecedented material prosperity: "You've never had it so good." It was the swinging
sixties in pop music, and the Beatles and the Rolling Stones
molded a generation. The seventies inevitably followed with
a self-centered determination to do "what I want," with no
absolutes and no holds barred. The eighties saw a growing
reaction against such free-for-all attitudes, and there was a
swing back to a firmer, indeed, harder mood. The materialism of the previous decades had never been questioned,
and the boom in the mideighties created a hard approach to
getting money, without too much principle and with little
compassion for the not-so-fortunate. The crash at the end of
the decade brought realism—and a sharpening disillusionment with money, materialism, and anything too definite in
any context.

At the beginning of the nineties, therefore, there is a
much more open attitude to what really matters, to people
and their needs, to other and all points of view, to spiritual
experience, to possibilities of international peace, to concern
for the environment, to new things and new places and new
people. There are other trends too—the flip side of openness, seen in those who close in on themselves and dismiss
or despise others. There is a strong nationalism—even fas-
cism—in many countries. There is tribalism, both literally in
African countries and among groups of people who, often
violently, enforce their presence, their philosophy, or their
power on others.

These general trends have created a religious atmosphere intriguingly similar to the world of the Mediterranean
in the first-century AD. In particular, the city of Athens seems
to have been in a mood of much the same kind when the
Apostle Paul visited it (Acts 17:16-34). It is worth learning
from him the way he made the gospel available and acceptable (in the right sense) to the Athenians.

We notice immediately that Paul's time in Athens was
unplanned: he was there on a break from his hectic life,

waiting for his friends and colleagues to arrive from northern Greece. So Luke's account is of "unintentional," off-the-cuff evangelism by a man whose entire life had been turned inside out and who was always, intentionally and unintentionally, concerned for those outside the Kingdom of God.

Athens was a city living on its past reputation: the cradle of democracy, the matrix of Greek philosophy, the center of literature, a city full of magnificent buildings and sculptures. But most of this was in the past. Philosophy had deteriorated into an elaborate intellectual exercise, not a search for the truth. Paul noted the following four things about the Athenians.

First, they were *idolatrous*—the city was "full of idols." There was temple after temple, dedicated to the worship of a different god or goddess. These were places of worship—the worship of idols. By substituting worship of the Creator with worship of things created, Athenians had also descended into crass immorality. Their art reflected their beliefs and their behavior—culturally and aesthetically superb, but morally and spiritually ugly and empty. Our own modern cities are much like Athens. Modern art reflects the meaninglessness, hopelessness, violence, and obscenity of our society.

Athenians were also *curious*: they were always wanting to hear something new. Life was boring without some sort of novelty, and two main philosophies of life guided their thinking. The Stoics saw the deity as an invisible, fiery vapor, of which individual souls were like little sparks. This fire interpenetrated all things. At death, the soul was reabsorbed into the world-soul. The key Stoic concept was *fate*: we are at the mercy of vast impersonal forces. We must grit our teeth, keep a stiff upper lip, be reasonable, accept things as they are, and exercise self-control.

The Epicureans believed in the gods, but that they were not interested in human affairs. The soul dissolves at death into the atoms that compose it: there is no future to dread or to desire. The chief aim is to relieve life of all fear and anxiety, especially about death. The key Epicurean concept was *chance*. The world and the universe are one gigantic "fluke." Therefore, pleasure is all that matters; let's get the most out of life, this life, because there is nothing else. Tranquility is the most prized possession. At its lowest, the Epicurean's philosophy was "Eat, drink, and be merry, for tomorrow we die."

Finding modern parallels to these old philosophies is not difficult. They are as universal as the sun, sea, and stars. There is an aching void in those who, inasmuch as they give the meaning of life much thought at all, believe either in fate or in chance.

The third characteristic Paul discovered about the Athenians' way was that they were very *religious*. Worship came naturally to them. They were pantheists, syncretists, universalists. The attitude seemed to be, take any number of gods, mix them up, and take your pick—you will come out fine in the end, anyway. Paul picks up this religious bent in explaining that the one true God made us to "feel after him and find him" and that "he is not far from each one of us." When Paul began to speak about Jesus and the Resurrection, however, they assumed he was introducing two more gods into the arena—Jesus, a male god, and Anastasis (Greek for resurrection), His female counterpart and concubine. So their immediate reaction was to combine these two with all the rest—a healthy warning that our familiar (to us) God-talk can be totally misheard by our listeners.

Lastly, Paul was clear that Athenians were *ignorant*, and he set about preaching to them "the unknown God," whom they "ignorantly worship." God does not dwell in temples; He does not need our gifts; He made both us and the world we live in. We are His offspring, and we must not make any image of God. Paul spoke in this basic way because Athenians were ignorant about God, which is very much the situation today: People's ignorance about God is almost breathtakingly total. We have to go back to square one in many cases. We cannot assume any real knowledge of Jesus — indeed, we cannot even assume that the concept of *God* carries any significance.

Unlike Athenians then, people today are the product of *pure paganism*. Athenians behaved and believed in a way that is often described as pagan, but they were in fact very religious. Pure paganism has been most aptly summarized by the historian Edward Gibbon, who, in his book *The Decline and Fall of the Roman Empire*, describes paganism as a time "when the philosophers think all religions are equally false, the people think all religions are equally true, and the politicians think that all religions are equally useful." In the 1990s in most Western nations, that is an accurate description of our religious climate.

The encouraging sign is that people are increasingly wanting to find and know the truth. One of the biggest challenges we face as Christians is to hold up Jesus as the Truth in a nonaggressive, compassionate, clear, listening way, so that those who seek the truth can see the difference between Jesus and other paths. We can no longer boldly declare the gospel in a take-it-or-leave-it fashion. We need to know the claims and counterclaims of other religions, so that we give a reasoned apologetic for Jesus.

The way Paul achieved this in Athens is edifying and important to us in our own apologetics. There is no space to look at his summarized sermon in detail, but three lessons stand out. First, he starts where his listeners are — by referring to what is happening in Athens, noting what has struck him, and beginning with what is familiar to them. Second, he scratches where they itch — by talking of a Creator who has fashioned us all, who gives us life and breath and everything, who is not miles away but can be reached, in whom we live and move and have our being, and to whom we owe our very existence.

Third, Paul stresses what they need to hear—by emphasizing what they ought *not* to think, and then underlining essential gospel truths. We will look at Acts 17:30-31 in some detail. The passage reads as follows: "The times of ignorance God overlooked, but now he commands all men everywhere to repent, because he has fixed a day on which he will judge the world in righteousness by a man whom he has appointed, and of this he has given assurance to all men by raising him from the dead." We will show the importance of this passage by dissecting it phrase by phrase:

The times of ignorance—other ways of thinking about God are not so much corrupt as out of date and ignorant

God overlooked—that is, winked at, turned a blind eye to; God is not intent on blitzing people into hell

But now—since Jesus: He is the hinge of history

He commands—it's an order, not an option

All men everywhere—wherever and whenever they live

To repent—that is, to change their whole way of thinking

Because he has a fixed day—the world will come to an end when God says so

On which he will judge the world—that is, we are accountable for our lives

In righteousness—He knows everything and this is righteous judgment

By a man — historical and human

Whom he has appointed — this is God's decision and choice

And of this he has given assurance — this is not dreamed up: there is solid evidence

To all men — not just a few "in the know," but through the few made universally accessible

By raising him from the dead — that's the miracle, and there is the uniqueness

That is the way Paul, an inside-out man if ever there was one, went about his evangelism in Athens. The reactions were mixed: some mocked, some procrastinated, some believed. There will always be such mixed reactions. That is why we must understand the religious atmosphere in which we are living, but never measure what is appropriate by positive results alone.

ABSORB THE SPIRITUAL HISTORY

Our third priority, in turning the church inside out, is to *absorb the spiritual history* of the area. This has several perspectives, wherever we live. For example, it is important to retrace the footsteps of Christians who have prayed, worshiped, worked, and witnessed in our neighborhood down through the decades, or even the centuries. How was the Christian church first established and by whom? What significant events or personalities have shaped the presence of Christians in this area? Have there been striking or seminal occasions leading to revival or division or expansion or retrenchment, for example?

Such elementary, local church history holds valuable clues, both for understanding and for building our spiritual heritage. It is worth having such history tackled by reasonably objective, if sympathetic and shrewd, observers. We recently asked a Cambridge University history graduate, a member of the congregation, to consult all local records he could unearth in order to compile a comprehensive report on the buildings locally that had been used or owned by the church.

His report, which was painstaking and detailed, brought to light any number of hitherto forgotten facts, many of which have stood us in good stead in establishing a stronger presence in the community. More than that, we pinpointed significant trends and emphases in the life of the church under previous ministers—all of which shed fascinating light on the spiritual ethos of the church. These characteristics became part of the spiritual fabric of the neighborhood and of the congregation. Like anything inherited, they can come to dominate current thinking and thereby dictate present behavior. Tradition has this double-edged impact on any church or community: It can be a rich vein for tapping into our spiritual resources, or it can degenerate into a veritable prison.

At worst, this spiritual history exercises almost a supernaturally powerful control over the life of a congregation. I think of one city-center church that has a long history of dominant individuals in positions of lay leadership. From these strong personalities have come important ministries of evangelism, social and political involvement, medical and civic impact on the city and the nation. A fairly laissez faire approach to these people and these ministries over a number of years, without any significant pastoral oversight or commitment to a united vision and to appropriate cooperation, brought its own painful legacy of disintegration, mutual suspicion, and alienation.

No amount of energy, prayer, and discussion—even to

the extent of special commissions for reconciliation—succeeded in resolving the impasse. Eventually the situation had to be addressed publicly in authoritative prayer, in the context of the congregation at worship, along the lines of our Lord's own instructions about binding and loosing in Matthew 18:18-20. The plain procedure for reconciliation in the preceding verses had been exhaustively pursued over the years in this church. It became clear that spiritual forces of darkness had established, not merely a foothold, but a stranglehold. This was spiritual warfare, not simply church discipline.

The combination, in Matthew 18:15-20, of a three-stage process toward reconciliation coupled with a clear declaration of authority in a church for binding and loosing indicates the close link between human sin and spiritual forces of evil. The real presence of the Lord Himself provides the necessary impetus to the gathered church at prayer in such an intractable situation—"Where two or three are gathered in my name, there am I in the midst of them" (18:20).

Our area's spiritual history might tell us of more blatant Satanic activity. It is well-known and well-documented that places, including buildings and outdoor sites, can become infested with dark forces. A local real estate agent telephoned me some time ago on behalf of a purchaser of a nearby property. It was being renovated by a team of builders, who lived on site because they came from another part of the country. After a series of weird experiences during the night—cupboards banging, windows opening, floorboards creaking, rooms going cold and clammy—the team of tough, rough young men refused to continue. They were terrified. We spent thirty minutes as a staff team praying, singing, sharing the gospel with the builders. We went through the whole house, directly binding the powers of darkness and expelling them in each infested area. It had become apparent that the property had had a history of tragedy and mayhem.

We have not exactly offered the services of the church to local real estate agents, whenever such a spiritual history comes to light; but the amount of Satanic infestation and influence, especially in areas with a long history, is considerable. The impact of the gospel needs to be brought to bear in such cases and in such ways.

This is especially true if occultism is established in the area — either through spiritism or witchcraft or any religious activity that taps into the powers of darkness. To remain ignorant of what has been going on over the years may well result in a very limited impact by the Church of Jesus Christ. Indeed, if the church feels that all its best efforts are somehow frustrated and doomed to failure, it may well be important to establish the spiritual history of the area before attempting any further initiatives in outreach.

It is surprising, in one sense, how the spiritual history comes to the surface. We have discovered that striking insights come through intercession. This can sometimes be the fruit of individuals at prayer. More often it comes when a group called and committed to intercession consistently smothers the neighborhood in prayer. The Lord seems to give insight about a particular building or family.

Another effective way of gaining insight is walking the streets in twos and threes, silently or quietly praying for each house or block as you go. Fascinating and determinative insights have come into the minds of such "prayer walkers."

Now this can all be used a bit obsessively and needs to be taken with a pinch of salty self-deprecation. It is important to mix careful research with prayerful insight. Such a ministry should not be talked about widely, let alone trumpeted publicly in the community. It does, nevertheless, lead to opportunities that open up only to such bold and sensitive initiatives.

At the very least we need to note the ups and downs of different churches in our area, as well as the influence of particular people with religious allegiance or convictions in local business, commerce, industry, education, and politics. The "feel" of a town or city can be signally affected, for better or for worse, by the way power has been thus exercised in a religious context. Wealthy benefactors and/or employers have often influenced the spiritual history over many generations.

This kind of influence becomes most significant if there has been any background of heretical, unorthodox, or cult impact. The presence of Freemasonry, with its tentacles of secrecy and manipulation, also needs to be taken into account. Any history of violent death, either through murder or suicide, invariably leaves traces of darkness and depression, not simply in the immediate family or in subsequent residents of the premises where the events took place, but also permeating a community.

The spiritual history of any area is a hodgepodge of facts, fancies, and fears. The good needs to be underlined and affirmed; the less good needs to be closely examined; the evil needs to be identified and driven out. There is such a thing as a clear and clean spiritual atmosphere. I remember well a Christian worker in Chile talking about the remarkable response to the gospel among certain segments of the population. Results were unprecedented—not just large numbers of people turning to Christ, but whole communities en masse and overnight converted from powerful animism to living faith in Jesus Christ. One determinative factor, he felt, was sixty or seventy years of steady preaching of the gospel in the open air up and down the country—the atmosphere had been cleared.

Is this something of what Paul meant when he spoke about the impact of the church's preaching? "To me . . . this grace was given, to preach to the Gentiles the unsearchable riches of Christ, and to make all men see what is the plan of the mystery hidden for ages in God . . . that through the church the manifold wisdom of God might now be made known to the principalities and powers in the heavenly places" (Ephesians 3:8-10). The apostle seems to see his own ministry of preaching and that of the church as a whole in two ways—making God's plan plain to human beings and making God's wisdom plain to spiritual beings, including especially "the spiritual hosts of wickedness." These beings contaminate places and communities. They bitterly resist God, Jesus, the Holy Spirit, the Church. They need to be forced, through prayer and preaching, to relinquish their grip on people and places. Then the gospel can have a free rein in a clean atmosphere.

PENETRATE THE LOCAL COMMUNITY

The fourth priority in turning the church inside out is to *penetrate the local community*. Our first three priorities are fundamental ways of preparing the ground, mainly by turning over the soil of our own hearts and minds so that God can Himself use us more effectively. Now we need to look imaginatively at the ways we can express our faith and discipleship together in the locality—not by occasional forays to blitz people with the message, but by being creatively involved in and committed to the community life of our neighborhood.

It would be a simple matter to concentrate on the risks of unwary involvement—for example, risks of compromise, contamination, or confusion. Let us rather consider some of the ways that we can become more effective. It is worth reminding ourselves that God Himself, in coming to rescue us from our situation, did not send messages, arrange the occasional visit, or hold a two-week crusade. He became one of us, one with us, to serve us, humbling Himself, despised and rejected, wounded and bruised in complete identification. So it must be important to reexamine the ways and means we use to commend this gospel of a God who saves by stooping and dying. If the medium is not the whole message, it is certainly the factor that either validates or invalidates what we are trying to say.

One of the most striking aspects of the ministry Jesus exercised was the amount of time He spent in people's homes and, in particular, at parties. When He was not with the crowds in the open air, He was invariably enjoying someone's hospitality. More often than not, the home and the hospitality belonged to someone either outside the circle of disciples or new to discipleship. This somewhat surprising socializing by the Lord is obvious once we have noted it, but it is still worth spelling out the record in the gospels.

In Luke's Gospel, for example, Jesus' first general healings took place on a specially memorable Sabbath day in the home of Simon Peter's mother-in-law. His teaching ministry, which at times took place in synagogues or in the Temple of Jerusalem, seemed to move naturally between outdoors and indoors. For example, He was teaching a large crowd in one particular home in Capernaum, when a paralyzed man was lowered to Him through a hole in the roof. This incident was followed by a great party in the house of Matthew, who invited all his colleagues in the tax office to meet his new Master.

Similar parties are mentioned by Luke—in the house of Simon the Pharisee, at the home of a second Pharisee, at dinner with a ruler of the Pharisees. Jesus insists on being a guest in the affluent Jericho penthouse of Zacchaeus. The Apostle John mentions that the first "sign" Jesus performed was at a wedding party. He was in and out of many people's homes, bringing healing and teaching—indeed, even raising the dead.

He apparently ignored social conventions and shibboleths in such environments, neither observing fussy washing habits nor keeping the conversation on safe topics. He was impervious to the niceties of socialites. He ignored taboos about places of honor, titles, and right or wrong people to invite. He rejected "tit-for-tat" hospitality. Yet He was relaxed in His enjoyment of the social whirl, even being accused of being "a glutton and winebibber," as well as acquiring a reputation for spending a good deal of His time in the company of prostitutes and property sharks.

In a culture renowned for the significance it attached to hospitality, not least to its code of conduct and etiquette in such matters, Jesus moved with distinctive ease and striking impact. He was — or appeared to be — the one person everyone wanted to have at his or her party. He might not have guaranteed its success, but He certainly made every such occasion unforgettable. Whatever was on the menu, Jesus added the salt — by His presence, His words, and His behavior.

There was more to it, of course, than simply finding yourself at the most interesting and memorable parties in town. Jesus Himself nailed that shallow deception. He likened the Kingdom of God, on more than one occasion, to a great party — with God Himself as host. At one particular party, He was in conversation with a man about entry into the Kingdom. He made a telling point about those who take part in social events, but without any spiritual awareness, by saying,

> "Then you will begin to say, 'We ate and drank in your presence, and you taught in our streets.' But he will say, 'I tell you, I do not know where you come from; depart from me, all you workers of iniquity.' There you will weep and gnash your teeth, when you see Abraham and Isaac and Jacob and all the prophets in the kingdom of God and you yourselves thrust out. And men will come from east and west, and from north and south, and sit at table in the kingdom of God. And behold, some are last who will be first, and some are first who will be last." (Luke 13:26-30)

Clearly, we have an inside-out pattern in our Lord's involvement in the social life of His community. Each area and country has its own patterns of hospitality. We need to find the most appropriate way for our own neighborhood. If Jesus' own practice is anything to go by, one of the keys is accepting invitations even more than giving them; that is, being ready (and having our diaries freed up) to go into the homes of unbelievers, and to talk about the Kingdom of God on territory that is familiar to them rather than to us.

We recently had a good example of this in London. Eight members of the church decided to organize a dinner in a local hotel with a focus on golf. An international woman golfer recently converted to Christ and agreed to be interviewed after the meal, and the chaplain to the European men's circuit gave a talk. Each one of the eight Christians found two other Christians. Each trio invited five uncommitted or unconverted friends to round out each table of eight. There were seventy-two people at the dinner, of whom two-thirds were not Christians. The venue was familiar and acceptable to the latter, and the proportion of Christians to nonChristians unthreatening. The atmosphere was relaxed; the talk and the interview were uncompromising; the conversations direct and to the point. Nobody left until 11:15 p.m., and the opportunity to respond further was clear, but low-key.

This kind of dinner party is a central-London example of Jesus' social ministry. If each local church invested, both financially and in human resources, in appropriate initiatives along similar lines, very many people—who are at present out of reach—would taste the life and the message of the church of Christ. It needn't be such an organized event, nor involve such large numbers, but we do need to work hard to turn the social life of our church inside out. In particular, we need to follow the example of Jesus in going out to where people are and where they feel comfortable. Almost by definition this means going places where we will probably feel uncomfortable. However, it is surprising how exciting it is to find spiritual hunger and thirst being articulated by people who would hardly darken the doors of a church building, and might even hesitate to open up on territory that feels strange to them, like a Christian's home.

There are many other ways of turning the life of the church out into the local community. Prevailing conditions, needs, and opportunities will suggest different approaches. For example, we live in an area of London that is flooded with visitors, commuters, and tourists. We are a couple of blocks from Victoria Station, and even closer to the main bus station, which serves the whole country and Europe. Food and drink are paramount needs. So we converted a church hall in a prime location—opposite the bus station—into a coffee bar and restaurant. Although the clientele is transient, we see this as a unique opportunity to preach the gospel. We employ a full-time evangelist to sit at tables and "gossip the gospel." Through a nationwide Christian agency, we can put people in touch with a local church if they wish to take things further.

The work is demanding, difficult, and at times danger-ous, because all sorts find their way to such a venue in the middle of a huge metropolis like London. We see it as another way of providing hospitality and a home-away-from-home for people on the move. It is rather like the way Jesus and His disciples mingled with the crowds on their pilgrimage to the capital to celebrate the great festivals. Today, London is one perpetual pilgrimage and one forever festival.

London is not only a metropolis, it is also a network of villages. Each area has its own center of meeting, focus of interest, desire for community. Traditionally and histori-cally, the parish church provided this sense of togetherness, although most churches have gradually allowed themselves to become irrelevant and pushed to the margins of the community.

We have sensed the need and the call to recover our traditional place in the community. We spent some time listening to and learning from local residents and shopkeepers. We heard what they wanted the local church to be and provide. After careful listening, sifting, and praying, we realized that the church (people and building) ought to act again as the heart of the community. Two particular events proved extremely important.

First, in conjunction with the shopkeepers and traders in local streets, we organized a street fair around Christmas. Food and drink were featured, along with stalls selling a wide range of goods and products. Clowns clowned, dancers danced, minstrels minstrelled, actors acted, and celebrities celebrated. Probably a couple thousand people have attended each of the three held in recent years. At the request of the community, Christmas carols were sung either in the street or in the church building. The impact of such an event cannot be measured, but the goodwill toward the church and the accessibility of Christians to nonChristians were both increased significantly.

The other initiative was to plan a concert in the church for the community — of as high a quality as we could achieve, with a strong flavor and involving mainly Christian performers. Church members used it as an opportunity to invite friends and neighbors to pre- or post-concert parties. These concerts — there have been two so far — have again acted as a rallying point for the local community in the middle of a vast depersonalized city.

Most churches develop their own range of activities along similar lines. I suppose my conviction and plea can best be summarized as follows: *Let us rigorously pursue a pattern of church life that is ruthlessly turned inside out, asking ourselves all the time how the love and light of Christ can be made as accessible as possible to those living and working around us.* It is risky, but it is rewarding. It is a vulnerable way to go, but it is a vital way. Above all, it is the Master's way.

EXPECT PEOPLE TO BEAR TESTIMONY

The other three priorities for turning the church inside out can be dealt with more briefly. The fifth tactic is to *expect people to bear testimony*. We have depended too long on the evangelist and the preacher. They have their place—but it is the ordinary disciple alone who has the most everyday, natural, close contact with unbelievers. Each disciple should be encouraged, enabled, and expected to tell his or her story of Jesus.

There are a number of most helpful courses to equip us to take the message out and about, usually as part of the evangelistic program of the local church and working to a strategy of outreach into the community. Many of these courses are of proven value and can be fully recommended. I am not, however, thinking of this kind of approach. Rather, we need to equip each and every disciple to talk (in daily encounter with colleagues, friends, and neighbors) about the relevance of Jesus Christ in his or her own life. Although there are basic principles and elementary instructions to bring to bear on this, it is crucial not to turn it into a package deal with a one-two-three approach.

The "story telling" needs to be firmly applied to—and arise out of—the daily experiences at work and at home of each believer. The believer is not so much giving his or her testimony, as ready "to account the hope that is in [him or her]" (1 Peter 3:15), whenever the opportunity is presented. So it is not a matter of pressing a button and out comes a testimony. It is a matter of keeping in living touch with Christ, learning to walk with Him day by day, and speaking clearly about Him.

I recently heard of a senior executive at a board meeting, where the directors were discussing a particular dilemma in a sector about which this man, a Christian, was unskilled and uninvolved. As those responsible seesawed their way around this very difficult situation, the Christian quietly prayed for the wisdom of God to come into the discussion. During a lull in the conversation, with the whole meeting at a loss what to do, he felt constrained to make a comment he knew had been inspired by the Holy Spirit: it was simply not within his province or capacity to make such a judgment. The words unlocked the dilemma and a solution was quickly seen, agreed to, and implemented.

Later the same day, one of his colleagues expressed amazement that this man could have been so shrewd and incisive in such a specialized sector of the company's business. "How did you come up with it?" he asked. The Christian explained that, while the others debated back and forth, he was praying, and God seemed to drop the words into his mind and mouth. "That's the kind of God I'm interested in. . . . Tell me more," was the reply.

If every disciple of Christ operated in a very similar way, open to God's wisdom and guidance in each new situation, the life of the church would truly be turned inside out. It underlines once more that the prime task of a local church is to equip every believer to carry on an effective, Christ-centered ministry in his or her daily life, instead of investing so much energy in helping a few to run the ministry of the church, with the lament that there are so few "really committed" people. Perhaps there are actually many, many committed Christians in our local churches, the problem being our unwillingness to hone and to channel that commitment into their daily life and work.

TARGET THE YOUNG PEOPLE

The sixth priority in turning the church inside out is to *target the young people.* By young people I mean those who are between the ages of fifteen and twenty-five, because they are the ones most notable by their absence from most local churches. A few, proportionately, are reached through specialist agencies, but that leaves the huge majority of fifteen- to twenty-five-year-olds in the spiritual wilderness. This is a specialized ministry that almost certainly needs specialists. It undoubtedly requires special skills, special grace, special resilience, special support. Those aspects are outside the scope of this book. They are well documented and readily available.

I am more concerned with attitudes, awareness, and availability. Anybody out of touch or sympathy with the contemporary youth scene (as I personally find myself now at risk of becoming) develops certain attitudes that, if concentrated at the heart of a local church, can switch young people off spiritually in a devastating, if not fatal, way. One major factor is music.

I regularly thank the inventor of the Walkman. As a father of four children, now between the ages of eighteen and twenty-three, I would gladly canonize the inventor of a gadget that has shielded my ears and my sanity from the worst excesses of contemporary music making. I now realize, however, that such technology has also insulated me from the single most important ingredient of today's younger generation.

It is now necessary for the church to accept, in whatever way and to whatever degree turns out to be appropriate, that the musical aspects of Christian worship have to take in realistically both the "feel" and the technological sophistication of modern music. This is a topic fraught with difficulty and taut with emotive, indeed passionate, convictions. The traditional organ, piano, choir, even guitar and music group—these are all not so much under threat of extinction as facing the reality of competition that is not going to go away.

Unless we are positively open to this, we will not win contemporary young people to Christ and His Church, and we are likely to lose those we have, or cause these to become alienated from and ineffective witnesses among their own generation. The only alternative scenario with any positive aspects is to see an exclusive youth church emerging without any interaction with the rest of the church.

To target the young people is costly and full of pitfalls. But I have a suspicion that this is where the heart of God beats with aching compassion. We had been praying for two years or more for an effective opening into the lives of local young people. Then God brought them, without any previous contact, to an evening service one winter Sunday. About twenty lads literally came down the aisle on skateboards and roller skates after the service had started. That amazing invasion heralded three or four years of painstaking friendship, mainly among teenage boys from Muslim backgrounds.

We cannot report roaring success. Indeed, almost the opposite is true. But if we are open and available, God is certainly longing to bring such young people across our path—or take us across theirs.

WORK TOWARD CHURCH PLANTING

The last priority in turning the Church inside out is simply stated, or restated from an earlier chapter, as follows: *work toward church planting*. In other words, do not let us be satisfied with a plan for church growth that increases our own numbers, facilities, programs, personnel, and reputation. Let us take seriously the primary nature of the Church as the family of God and as the Body of Christ. Both the family and the body are meant to grow. When they are healthy they do grow.

They are not, however, intended to proliferate unendingly. Rather, the family is meant to reproduce, to multiply by division; the body is meant to be fruitful once it has come to maturity. If a local church holds to these two biblical images of its essential calling, it will spontaneously find itself turned inside out. It will constantly be looking to increase, not merely by more and more numbers or members, but by reproducing or transplanting its whole life in another neighborhood, or elsewhere in the same neighborhood.

A much-quoted aphorism about the church holds particularly true when viewed in this context: It is "the only club that exists for nonmembers." A local church has been brought into being, and enabled to grow, in a community with the express intention of serving that community in the name of Jesus Christ. In the words of Emil Brunner, "The church exists by mission as a fire exists by burning." To use a third quotation, "The church that lives to itself dies by itself."

These truths are as valid for local churches with large numbers as for those with only a few. We need consistently and courageously to steer Christians away from any attempt to turn the Church into a safe house, a place of refuge, a haven from which no effort is made to face the high seas again. Only as we receive the grace to be turned inside out, paradoxically and almost unconsciously, do we find we are safe, secure, settled, and satisfied.

✳   ✳   ✳

1. How can the life of your church be turned more inside out?

2. Do you have a thorough knowledge of the community and geographical area in which you are placed? What about its "spiritual history"?

3. Do the people in your church have a good grasp of fundamental Christian truth as it is relevant to our contemporaries? Can *you* communicate Christian truth to your friends and colleagues? Use the Apostle Paul's sermon at Athens to guide you.

4. Does the party-going example of Jesus give you so[me] clues about your own lifestyle as witness to Jesus? How so?

5. What are you doing for and with the young people of your area?

me

CHAPTER TEN

EMBRACING
CHANGE AND GROWTH

New Year's Day—the middle of winter here in the Pyrenees in southwestern France. The sun is shining brightly and there is a chill in the air. The lush foliage and pastures of our little valley, which we first saw in the height of summer, have long since disappeared. Instead of a riot of different colors, the trees are brown and bare. Each tree stands alone, stripped and solitary. A bird sings, a fly buzzes, a cockerel crows, a dog barks, a hawk circles. Beyond that there are not many signs of life. Our little rock garden, rescued from oblivion in the spring and producing signs of hope in the summer, is now bare and barren.

And yet . . . and yet we know the trees will bud and blossom, the flowers will grow and bloom, and there will be new lambs to swell the depleted flock. The fields will produce corn and barley, and the vines will once more be heavy with grapes. The crocus, dahlia, tulip, and daffodil will all appear once again. If we judged simply by appearances, and if we chose to evaluate only at one time of the year, we would make fundamental mistakes and, in fact, get the whole picture entirely wrong.

The same is true in the life of a local church. As in nature, so in our new nature as God's community. As in creation, so in God's new creation. We call the different stages in this growth the seasons of the year. We rely on them because they come around in a regular cycle: spring,

215

summer, autumn, and winter. In extreme climates these seasons sometimes merge or disappear. In more equable climates we come to appreciate more and more the rich diversity within and between each season. It is important to observe and relish certain distinctives in the cycle of a local church's life. God is both Creator and Re-Creator, the Author of all life both physical and spiritual. It seems He has determined that such a cycle of change and growth has been written into all that He creates.

WINTER

Winter in a local church. Everything can look lifeless, drab, and without hope—especially in comparison with what has happened in the past days and what might be happening in other churches. The vitality seems to be missing; the sparkle and the zest have disappeared. There is no outward evidence—or even symbol—of new life. The small things seem to us so precious that we treasure them; they are the only evidence that something might still be happening . . . or might start to happen.

When we feel like this and are tempted to depression, if not despair, it is good to remember that winter is not merely inevitable but necessary if there is to be growth. A church, any more than the land, cannot exist in perpetual summer. It is important not to become completely absorbed by even a long winter, to the point where we lose sight of what will emerge in God's own time. His work is necessarily hidden from our eyes, because it is going on steadily beneath the surface.

The Holy Spirit, the Author and Giver of life, quietly carries on this concealed work in the hearts and minds of believers, preparing the people of God for the time and the ministry of His own choosing. This fact is as definite and as certain as the fact that spring follows winter.

We all want the outward evidence too quickly, without

appreciating and relishing the hidden work of the Spirit. There are definite advantages to the marks of winter in a church. We can enjoy the small things, the contribution of each individual, the sharp nip in the spiritual atmosphere, the clearer vision unobscured by the haze of success, the call to live by faith in what God will do rather than by sight of all the visible signs of growth around us. It is good, also, to spend more time together in small groups "around the fire" in worship and in God's Word, rather than rushing around in a multitude of activities. In spiritual winter the days are shorter and the nights are longer. But that means we may enjoy the sun while we can.

Pruning

It is, of course, true to say that winter — and winter's experiences — does not simply happen. We do not move from autumn to winter overnight, although it might sometimes seem like it. One essential preparation for winter, which is actually also a preparation for spring, is *the act of pruning*. If we believe that a tree or a shrub is going to produce more fruit or flowers next year, then we have no hesitation in reaching for the pruning shears. Pruning requires skill, but it is absolutely crucial to growth.

When the Lord Jesus called His Father the true Gardener or Husbandman or Vinedresser, He was highlighting this vital work in God's creation, the Church. Throughout both Old and New Testaments the people of God are likened to a vine. In John 15, Jesus Himself is the true vine and we, His people, are the branches. Jesus fully commits Himself to bearing fruit for God. And He commits us in Him to bear fruit, fruit that will remain and fruit that will increase. For this fruitfulness to be properly effective, the vine has to be pruned. This pruning has to be applied to each individual branch. Any branch that bears fruit the Father prunes, "in order that it might bear more fruit."

There is one simple truth about this process, both in

the physical and the spiritual world: we cannot be pruned and bear fruit at the same time. The very experience of pruning commits us to a period of fruitlessness—not life-lessness, because the life is still within the branch. But a pruned branch that has life within it need not fear pruning: indeed, it should welcome it. So with a local church and each individual believer within it. It is good for us to be trimmed, to be cut back, to be stripped of outward success, and to be forced to rely on the Spirit of life within us. When individual members of a local church find themselves being thus pruned in their walk with Christ and in their daily witness, wise leaders will welcome this initiative by the Gardener/Vinedresser as a sure pointer from God toward a time of outward lack of fruit, leading to a time of growth far richer and far more rewarding.

Without doubt, such a time of pruning will also be a call from God to a church deliberately and decisively to cut back on activities and expansion plans. We are all so programed for "bigger and better" that we find such divine directives extremely painful. Our pride rebels. Our own ambitions resist the pruning shears and the One who holds them. We would be far wiser to take a pause, make time for quiet reflection, and reappraise everything happening in our church—with a view to excising anything that has not in recent months and years borne any fruit. Jesus remarked that such "branches" are "good for nothing," to be tossed in the fire and burned.

Embracing Winter

When, therefore, we become aware that God's pruning knife is in His hands and that our winter is approaching, we need carefully and humbly to make ourselves available to the Gardener. Let us allow Him freedom to cut back or cut off whatever He chooses. No single activity, program, or organization is sacrosanct. Winter is the time for quiet, hidden, private growth. We all *need* winter: individuals need winter;

churches need winter. Many churches and individuals fight against winter because they want perpetual summer.

It is, in fact, not surprising that some of the most extravagant versions of the "prosperity gospel" emanate from southern California, where the physical climate is anything but equable, where the sun is always shining and where winter is unknown, where spring and autumn are scarcely seen, where the desert has been forced to flourish by means of immense irrigation schemes. If people live in perpetual summer under constantly sunny skies, they come to believe that life is like that, that this kind of life is normal and natural, and that anything other than such conditions is wrong.

As in the physical world, so in the spiritual world. Instead of welcoming and valuing the distinctives of winter, as we have outlined them above, Christians who have adopted this "summer-only" mentality expect God always to make the sun shine on them. When the sun even goes behind a cloud or two, some Christians begin to assume that something has gone terribly wrong. Disappointments, reverses, failure become indicators of God's judgment or Satan's handiwork or both.

When this attitude prevails, Christians become completely thrown by constant or severe pressure. When the sun really goes in and the dark night of the soul overtakes them, there is nothing either in their experience or (even worse) in their theology to turn their eyes toward God. If God's blessing has been locked up in health, wealth, and happiness, where can the blessings come in sickness, poverty, and sadness?

Let us, then, learn to recognize and to rejoice in the blessings of winter. Within that discovery is an understanding that, whatever we do, it is always God who gives the life and the increase. It is by His timing and decision, not ours, that we find a local church to be enjoying the freshness of spring or the full fruit of autumn. Of one thing we can be sure: we will not reach spring without winter, and we will not know the fruitfulness of autumn without the steady sowing-in-hope of springtime.

Discerning the Cycle

In my own experience of four churches, this cycle and rhythm of the seasons has been apparent. Moreover, I have found it vital, now that I've noticed this divine process, to explain it to the people of God. Such interpretation of God's ways brings insight and hope. It also provides both a perspective on present events and a corrective to unhealthy attitudes of either success or failure. In these four churches the pace of change from one season to the next has varied. As in different physical climates, so in local churches the different seasons vary in length. The changeover time also varies in different churches and different climates.

For example, in Cape Town both autumn and spring are relatively short, but dramatic and impressive, often lasting only two or three weeks. In a particular Cape Town church, winter lasted three years, as more and more was cut back and removed. Spring flourished for a few months—with a plethora of burgeoning life—then we were into a long balmy summer that lasted for several years—growth, impact, success. Autumn with its mellow fruitfulness, but with its first frosts and piercing winds, eventually followed: people left the church for greener pastures, and divisions made themselves painfully apparent.

If, for whatever reason, we do not learn to move with this rhythm in the life of a local church, we may well find ourselves caught up in a process of activity, which may be busy or boring, but which is dictated merely by human factors and not by the Holy Spirit. For example, we need honestly to face the fact that some local churches are, not just outwardly lifeless, but actually dead. Winter—or summer—has killed them off: there is no spiritual life around at all. Equally, it is possible to have an intensely active and busy church, rushing around in frenetic circles and not going anywhere, with inner spiritual life.

In Oxford, I often feared we had become like this. Because there were large numbers of undergraduates and students of all kinds in the congregation, it was right and proper that we geared much of our ministry to their distinctive needs. These young people were in Oxford for a minimum of twenty-four weeks in the year, although the average was probably more like thirty weeks. They came to Oxford normally for three years and no more. We had evolved a program of ministry that was demonstrably successful by any reasonable criteria. We followed this, in effect, in a three-year cycle. We rolled into action in September and were in top gear by the start of the academic year in October. The three terms or semesters each year had a distinctive emphasis. The intention was to contact and catch young students at the outset of their university career and send them on their way, about three years later, rejoicing in God.

The church was, however, both student and nonstudent. The nonstudent members of the congregation were virtually forced to adapt to this admirable, but artificial, cycle—which was repeated every three years. It is likely that we never came to terms in any realistic way with God's own rhythm of life for His people as a whole in that church. A man-made process (the university system) dictated our life as the people of God.

TRANSFORMATION

This is an opportune moment to pause and remind ourselves that we are at this point looking at the process of *change* in a local church. So far in this chapter, we have considered the cycle and rhythm of the seasons in creation and re-creation. Growth and change are the heart of this. We have just noted the way that one local church, the one in Oxford, may well have allowed its own life to be determined largely by a process of change inherent in its own manmade environment, the university. Is this not a classic example, if it is an accurate analysis, of what the Apostle Paul warns us to watch for? Listen to these familiar words: "Do not be conformed to this world but be transformed by the renewal of your mind" (Romans 12:2).

We have become so accustomed to applying these words, rightly and relevantly, to our individual discipleship, that we forget that Paul wrote them "to all God's beloved in Rome, who are called to be saints" (1:7) — that is, to the local church in Rome. The last chapter of Romans is a long list of fraternal greetings from "all the churches of Christ" (16:16) to the church at Rome. It is not unreasonable, therefore, to conclude that Paul's famous and incisive instructions to Christians not to be conformed to contemporary trends and patterns of behavior, but to be transformed by the renewal of their thinking, are meant to challenge any way that local churches, in Rome or anywhere, fail to allow the Holy Spirit of the living God to move them away from the all-embracing clutches of our culture into the pattern of ongoing change undertaken by God in Christ.

Committed to Change

It is in this primary and foundational sense that the local church must be committed to change. The word translated "be transformed" in Romans 12:2 literally is "be metamorphosed" — that is, the very shape of our life together needs to be molded by God, not by the prevailing culture, environment, or society. So constant change is here to stay, for as long as we have not arrived at that perfection for which God laid hold of us in Christ. If this radical change is "the angel of the unchanging God," clearly we do well to look for it and, finding it, to welcome and rejoice in it. It is clearly no minor affair, because it involves nothing short of our being made and kept new — that is, our whole way of thinking about God, the world, the Church needs to be transformed. There is, therefore, no blueprint for a local church . . .butthereisthisconsistentcommitmenttoconstant, steady transformation.

When we look more closely at the way change is described in the New Testament, we appreciate more and more just how central it is to our life together as God's people. It begins and continues with a vision of God. Paul again epitomizes the nature of this transforming vision: "We all, with unveiled face, beholding the glory of the Lord, are being changed into his likeness from one degree of glory to another" (2 Corinthians 3:18). Paul is unequivocal in stating that "this comes from the Lord, who is the Spirit." As in a church the people of God focus their vision on the Lord Himself, not on events or personalities, God's Spirit Himself goes to work transforming them into the people they are intended by God to be. There will be no vision *from* God for a local church, unless and until it is developing such a vision *for* God.

Inner Change
I have found that God's people can face any organizational or outward change, so long as they know within themselves the reality of the Spirit's transforming power to make them steadily more and more like Christ. If, by contrast, they become conscious of the spiritual stagnation within their own souls, they are most unwilling to face up to change—and quite unable to unite in pursuing it. This factor is nothing more or less than one further example of the futility of social or structural change without an inner, spiritual experience of God's redeeming grace. Social activism of any kind is the kiss of death to a church, unless it is rooted deep in the very gospel of God—that is, in all that God has done for us in Christ. Equally, when the people of God are truly gripped and galvanized by the good news of Jesus Christ, there are few things that they, in the name of Christ, will not attempt and achieve.

Another New Testament perspective on change is provided, again by Paul, in the letter to the Philippians. He has just mentioned, with grief and shame, those whose minds are set on "earthly things" and "whose god is the belly." By contrast, he writes, "our citizenship is in heaven" (NIV). This other-worldly citizenship, when properly recognized and duly worked out, brings about complete transformation—even to the point where "the Lord Jesus Christ . . . will transform our lowly bodies so that they will become like his glorious body" (Philippians 3:20-21, NIV). That is change with a capital *C*, and it is all possible because of "the power that enables him to bring everything under his control." We are called and committed to change, to be changed, because we are in the hands of such a transforming Savior. It is, therefore, to betray our calling not to enter joyfully into change and transformation.

The depth and totality of this change is reinforced once more by Paul in another familiar passage in 2 Corinthians 5:17-21. The central theme of change in this passage is obscured by our English use of the words *reconcile* and *reconciliation*. The Greek root in the words thus translated means "other" or "different." Paul is explaining in this passage that, as in his own life, God has acted decisively through Jesus to make people different, so that they become in and through Christ "other" people altogether. "All this is from God," states Paul. The situation between human beings and God could not have been worse: alienation, hostility, separation, sin, death. But God went into action and changed the situation once and for all. He changed enemies into friends, transformed sinners into accepted children sharing His own righteousness. He did this by making Him, who knew no sin, to be sin for us (5:21). Now He is at work transforming us, "so that in him we might become the righteousness of God."

It must, surely, be irresponsible ever to call for change in the structures, organization, and programs of a local church, without this New Testament explanation of *inner* change and transformation being the heart of the matter. Paul is clear, for example, in this last passage, that such an immense act of salvation on God's part leaves us as God's people with both a message and a ministry of change — "God has entrusted/committed to us the message of reconciliation" (that is, of making people different and "other" people altogether). He has done this for us, and now He has given us the same ministry of reconciliation. So any Christian experiencing change and transformation is irretrievably and automatically involved in ministering change.

Paul, then, gives us at least these four key perspectives on change and transformation — transformation by the renewal of our minds, transformation through our vision of God, transformation of our bodies to be like the glorious body of the ascended Christ, and transformation as the very message and ministry in our calling to be disciples of God-in-Christ. These perspectives should form the basis of any call for change. Certainly, we can never endorse change for change's sake, but we can begin to look upon change as essential and exciting.

ENFORCED CHANGE

In the economy of God, much change among and within His people has the appearance of being forced upon us, rather than being directly welcomed. Something unpleasant or unexpected happens — and we have to change, or perish.

We have recently had a vivid and powerful example of this at our church in London. One of our three distinct congregations had been struggling for several weeks with alternative, less structured and formal, ingredients in our worship services — to go alongside, not to replace, more familiar material. We had gone this way and that on the leadership team, in a rather vain and "reinventing-the-wheel" attempt to please most of the people most of the time.

Suddenly, our worship services were interrupted for several weeks in succession by militant gay activists, who took them over with heckling, shrill whistles, placards, and mock prayers. At times there were thirty or more in the building, causing mayhem and not a little distress. It was, naturally, impossible to proceed with our orderly, rather formal, pattern of worship. We had to improvise, and we were not slow to recognize that the more informal songs of worship were very suitable for the special kind of spiritual conflict in which we were now engaged.

Much more could be said about these particular circumstances — the experience was a great change-and-growth one for the people of God as a whole, within which the appropriate and valuable place of more informal worship was self-evident. We had tried to impose a certain kind of change without properly engaging the spiritual lives of God's people. We would not have chosen the circumstances in which our choice of change began to backfire, but God's ways are not our ways.

Occasion for significant change in a church often comes, not surprisingly, when the leadership changes — especially if the main pastor moves on. I say this is not surprising, and yet it is never easy for a church to face up to the realities or the implications of change in such a situation. Indeed, there always seems to be an influential group of people in place at such times who definitely want no significant change at all, apart from a change of face in the pulpit and a change of name on the notice board.

Others will, more realistically, recognize the inevitability of change, but will try hard to keep it as small and as short-lived as possible. They are afraid of too much uncertainty due either to protracted delays or to new directions. Still others will see such a vacuum as their opportunity to bring in the change they have for many years wanted and worked for.

It is an extremely testing and challenging time, when so

much seems to be at stake, and when it is exceedingly hard to look to the Lord. My personal conviction is that a change of leadership is classically the time to expect both thorough examination and radical change. Both will be painful but, if the process is tackled with eyes alert and with genuine openness, the end result will be immense growth. People will move into greater responsibility than ever before. So far from this being a period of holding fire and standing one's ground, it can be a time for marked advance as the people of God. Any wrong reliance on human leadership will soon be made plain, as will the presence of personal agendas.

I personally know of several churches in recent years that have experienced long, protracted periods of doubt and difficulty, while looking for a successor to a highly success-ful and popular leader. Two or three years is not uncom-mon. I believe that God, in His wise compassion and clear determination, has kept the people of these churches "in the dark" about the right person *precisely because* He has wanted to do important things in their midst. Frustrations and fears have, in this sense, been part of God's guidance. The uncer-tainty over many months or years has been as much due to the guiding hand of God as the eventual moment of deci-sion. It is good for us to be checked by indecision, when decisiveness would be dangerous and self-motivated.

Although every local church needs the strong guidance of God, particularly during periods of transition, this is very necessary in strong and successful churches. We have already noted the danger, in such churches, of assuming that outward success is a guarantee of divine pleasure. Because God resists proud churches as well as proud individuals, we can expect such successful churches to have a tough time on occasions like the choice of a new leader. This may well be when a church enters into a long dark winter . . . but spring always awaits, often bringing with it a new kind of church altogether. We cannot forget that winter does mark the death of the old, in order that something new might emerge, even if there is a degree of continuity between the old and the new.

So, the kind of change and growth to which God is committed within His very self is death-into-life, not just once but as a rhythm in creation and re-creation. As we thus positively and gratefully cooperate with God in all that He is at work doing with us, so we discover "what is the will of God, what is good and acceptable and perfect" (Romans 12:2). Thus, being transformed and discovering God's will for our life together as the people of God go hand in hand; when we stop growing we stop discovering God's will. This underlines the fact that God's will is not a static formula hidden away in a secret place, but rather it is the heart of a Father who has chosen to make Himself known to us and delights to have us, as His sons and daughters, share His heart's desires and intentions. As we spend time with Him, we not only discover His will but also discover that we are becoming more and more like Him in our desires and intentions.

HEARING GOD'S CALL TO CHANGE

It remains to consider how a local church can reach the place of recognizing God's call to change and growth in a truly united way. If we accept the importance of the small-group network for practical growth in discipleship, and if we appreciate the value of shared decision making in a leadership team, we are in a position to see the whole church recognize, own, and pursue God's vision for its future. And it is vital that the whole church is involved in all three activities—recognizing, owning, and pursuing.

To recognize God's call to change, we must be more than mere receivers of a decision from others. As far as possible, the whole people of God needs to be aware of the responsibility for everyone to discern what God is saying. This means, simply but profoundly, that each individual needs to spend time with the Lord in prayer and in studying the Scriptures—in the conviction that God is able to lead His people into His will for His church with unity of purpose and harmony of spirit. If we do not believe it can happen, it certainly will not happen. But the Word of God assures us that the peace of Christ will be the referee in times of dispute and uncertainty; indeed, that peace is the actual calling and legacy of Christ to the body of believers (Colossians 3:15). So we do well to bring about a proper consultation process for possible changes in the Body of Christ.

If all are involved, in an appropriate way, in the process of discovering and recognizing the will of God, all will be able to own the will of God for themselves. It will not be a legalistic or less-than-responsible business of conforming to those who know best, but a joyful, wide-awake, expectant acceptance of the right way forward. We cannot overestimate the value and importance of such public ownership of God's priorities for a church. So we will be happy for such a process, leading to such united ownership, to take what might perhaps seem like an inordinate amount of time, effort, and consultation. The better the health of home groups and of shared leadership, the less protracted the process will actually be.

Once the significant membership of a church has actively embraced the process of recognizing and owning the vision of God for its growth and transformation, it will be highly motivated for pursuing it as time unfolds. Newcomers will need to be brought into the vision and into the history of its discovery, without pandering to the need in some to question its validity from the outset. It is not uncommon for strong personalities effectively to stymie God's vision for a church they have just joined.

For these priorities to be securely in place, we need a longer time scale in our minds than we might normally consider. For example, to discover, recognize, own, and pursue God's vision for a local church through one major stage of its developing life will probably take at least five years, except in most unusual circumstances. Most of us prefer clear, firm, unprotracted decision making: that is why we naturally opt for strong leadership from a few gifted people. Only later, when a congregation is at the stage of pursuing a particular course of action, do the problems begin to loom large and take over. We then reap the fruits of restricted consultation in the shape of foot shuffling and lack of commitment at the grass roots. The initial momentum fades; the motivation begins to evaporate; divisions begin to rear their heads. What looked like a very attainable goal seems light years away.

So it is advisable to look at change from a long-term perspective and, within that, to invest good time in the processes of wide consultation and decision making. If people know they have both been consulted and heard, they will usually be content with what the people of God as a whole decide to do. In general, change that is discerned and pursued by God's people together, through prayer, study of God's Word, awareness of the facts and in open discussion, will be both fruitful and glorifying to God. This is the people of God acting in the new community life of the Holy Spirit, in openness and taking risks, believing that, because this is our calling, "He who calls you is faithful, and he will do it" (1 Thessalonians 5:24).

✳   ✳   ✳

1. In which "season" do you think your church is living spiritually at this moment? Identify aspects of the four seasons in church life.

2. Do you think your church has allowed itself to become conformed to the cultural trends of the society around it? Why do you say that?

3. Does change excite, scare, exhaust, or sober you?

4. Is the internal change brought by God's Holy Spirit the key reality of your church's life together? Can you see evidence for this kind of change?

5. Can you think of examples in your church's life where God has used events and circumstances to bring about significant change? Describe them.

NOTES

Chapter One: Creating Community

1. Jean Vanier, *Community and Growth,* rev. ed. (London, England: Darton, Longman & Todd, 1989), pages 20-21.
2. Vanier, page 12.

Chapter Four: Keeping It Small

1. Gerhard Kittel, ed., *Theological Dictionary of the New Testament* (Grand Rapids: Eerdmans, 1965), 3: page 1036.

Chapter Five: Learning to Worship

1. C. S. Lewis, *Reflections on the Psalms* (London, England: Geoffrey Bles, 1958), page 92.
2. Lewis, page 85.
3. Lewis, pages 83-84.
4. Lewis, page 94.
5. Lewis, page 51.
6. Lewis, page 94.